Forgiveness,
the Passionate Journey

Forgiveness,
the Passionate Journey

Nine Steps of Forgiving
through Jesus' Beatitudes

Flora Slosson Wuellner

UPPER
ROOM BOOKS®
NASHVILLE

Library of Congress Cataloging-in-Publication Data
Wuellner, Flora Slosson.
    Forgiveness, the passionate journey: nine steps of forgiving through
Jesus' Beatitudes/by Flora Slosson Wuellner.
      p. cm.
    Includes bibliographical references.
    ISBN 0-8358-0945-5
    1. Forgiveness--Religious aspects--Christianity. 2. Beatitudes. I. Title.
BV4647.F55 W84 2001
241.5'3--dc21   2001017733

*Gratefully I dedicate this book
to those who prayed for my guidance in the writing.
You know who you are.
Without the help of your prayers,
this book could not have been written.*

Contents

Introduction

~

A sudden, mysterious, quite radical shift in our human consciousness has occurred since the turn of the millennium. This shift is an unprecedented, almost explosive concern for forgiveness, forgiveness asked for, forgiveness received, forgiveness exchanged, both communal and individual.

On my desk I have a stack of recent news articles from around the world. Pope John Paul II has expressed profound sorrow on behalf of the church for Jewish suffering at the hands of Christians. He has asked for forgiveness.

In Rwanda, Hutus and Tutsis are learning to pray together in evangelical churches, embracing, exchanging forgiveness for the hatred of centuries.

The Japanese prime minister officially apologized for many government-approved merciless actions during World War II.

Catholics and Protestants are meeting to pray together for peace in Northern Ireland, exchanging forgiveness for centuries of hurt.

Forgiveness

In September 2000, the head of the federal Bureau of Indian Affairs apologized for the agency's legacy of racism and inhumanity. This is the highest-ranking U.S. official ever to make such a statement regarding the treatment of Native Americans.

At the time of this writing an interracial group of lawmakers is preparing a resolution, to be presented to Congress, for an official apology by the United States for the enslaving of Africans. (This act should have come at least a century ago!)

I even have read an article about a big, friendly reunion (the first ever) between the formerly fiercely feuding clans of the Hatfields and McCoys!

These are only a few examples of public attempts at forgiveness. These efforts would have been inconceivable a generation ago.

Workshops about teaching and practicing forgiveness are taking place all over the country. There is even a widely publicized Forgiveness Week. We are urged first to forgive ourselves, then family, friends, other economic groups, other cultures and ethnic groups, political parties, and finally other nations. A day is allotted for each category!

An increasing number of books and articles, both religious and secular, urge us to forgive for the sake of our health, our longevity, our peace of mind. We are reminded that if we nourish resentment and hostility in our hearts, our immunity to disease is lowered and our relationships will suffer.

This sudden great shift of consciousness is almost breathtaking! And yet, as with any great mental and spiritual change, the faster it grows, the more devastatingly dangerous the change if mishandled. I am gratefully awed by this new intense focus on forgiveness, but at the same time I know that forgiveness is a perilous and volatile subject because it is so deeply intertwined with our communal and individual wounds, some of which extend back in time for hundreds of years. There is so much simplistic interpretation of forgiveness that almost completely overlooks the complexity of human pain and personality. So many questions and perplexities are barely looked at, let alone explored, perhaps *especially* in our Christian communities.

For example, forgiveness is rarely defined in a clear way. We use the word so much, but we do not really explain its meaning. Is forgiveness the same as acquiescence? Does forgiveness always imply reconciliation and restoration of former relationships?

How do we forgive a whole community, such as a dysfunctional family, an ethnic group, a whole nation? Is it possible to forgive what happened generations ago? Are we supposed to forgive on behalf of other people?

What do we *do* with our feelings of anger, hurt, sorrow, fear, when trying to forgive? Is forgiveness a onetime act of will? Is it a deepening process?

Can we set limits and borders within forgiveness? Can we leave another person or a community and still forgive? Can we love without liking? Is forgiveness possible at all if there has been severe, long-term abuse? Are there things which we should *not* forgive?

Does God really forgive everything? How do we forgive God for allowing such cruel abuse and inhumanity in the world?

Is it possible to forgive ourselves when we have wounded others? What does it mean to forgive ourselves? How is it done?

Forgiveness

Most of us have struggled with these and similar questions. I know I have. Over a long period I have slowly become aware of a big difference between healthy and unhealthy forgiveness and have been trying to discern just what creates that difference. During retreats, talks with others, much prayer, and a lot of reading and thinking, a book began to take shape. My editor agreed that a book on forgiveness would be timely. I struggled with the idea some more and finally prepared an outline. But something was missing, and I began to doubt if I were the right person to write this particular book after all.

Then one night a dream came. It was one of those rare dreams that are clear, powerful, significant, which I call guidance dreams. In the dream I was told God wanted me to write a book on the nine Beatitudes that open Jesus' Sermon on the Mount. "And write it with passion," I was firmly told. "Wait a minute," I said. "I've agreed with my editor that I'll write a book on forgiveness. That has to come first, I'm afraid."

Whoever was talking to me in the dream did not bother to argue. I woke up, got out of bed, went down to my study. I opened my Bible to Matthew 5 and read the nine great blessings. I knew them well, of course. We have all heard them read in church many times. But now I read them from a different perspective. Amazed, I realized that my forgiveness outline flowed, point by point, alongside those nine steps of deepening blessedness! Here was my book, already prepared. Jesus has already told us how to forgive.

Obviously, there are many ways by which to read, hear, and understand the Beatitudes. We find multiple meanings and insights in the scriptures because they are not dead legalism but are pulsing with life.

For example, we can read the Beatitudes from a communal perspective as the ways by which a communal body receives blessing from God and responds to God. Or we can read them from the moral justice and compassion angle as the ways God reaches through us to the poor, the vulnerable, the hungry, and the exploited.

We can find there also the deep individual ways of spiritual growth, as well as the ways of healing and release from addictions and other prisons of the spirit.

Alongside all these ways of hearing the Beatitudes, I found the path of healthy, empowered forgiveness of others and forgiveness of ourselves. So with excitement, as well as healthy trepidation, I began the adventure of writing this book. As I write, I realize again how much we all need one another in the exploration of this vast frontier of human consciousness—how much we need to share with one another, learn from one another, encourage one another.

As with all my books, I urge each reader to use the suggested healing meditation at the end of each chapter (beginning with chapter two) with deep respect for your personal needs. The area of our hurt, hostility, and healing is hot and holy ground!

Never push yourself or anyone else in these meditations. If you feel pain or anxiety increasing, leave the meditation at any point. Pray in some other way, go to sleep, quietly leave the room if a group is there, seek out a trusted friend and talk about what you feel, write in a journal.

Such meditations should not be substituted for any necessary professional therapy. I believe in prayer plus therapy, especially if the wound, abuse, anger, or fear is deep and longstanding.

Forgiveness

To be blessed means two things in scripture: It means to be happy, to be fulfilled. It also means to be empowered by God's love to undertake a task. The living Jesus Christ not only empowers us for healthy forgiveness but walks the path with us, enfolding us with God's compassion, praying through the pain "that my joy may be in you, and that your joy may be complete" (John 15:11).

CHAPTER ONE

Forgiveness: How Is It Possible?

~

With dignity and deep pain he shared his perplexity with me as we sat together in the retreat house chapel. "I love my mother and father. At least, I think I do. They did some fine things for me, and I'm grateful. But I simply can't forget those early years of nonstop criticism and severe punishment. They never spoke about anything I did right, only the wrong things. I grew up thinking that basically I wasn't a good person, even though I tried to do the right things and make them proud of me. I don't remember any hugs. I can't even remember if they ever said they loved me.

"Yes, I've had counseling, and I understand in my head that I'm a worthwhile person. And in my head I know *they* also came from homes where they were punished and criticized. In recent years they have made some attempts to come closer to me as they get older, and I've tried to do the same. I visit them, phone them, talk with them (though we've never talked about those early years), but that wall is still between us and I can't climb over it no matter how much I try. You notice I said I understand them and myself better in my head. But nothing seems to reach the hurt deep down in my heart."

This hurting, middle-aged man was a faithful church member and a devout Christian. He knew that Jesus taught forgiveness. He had read the books that told him how his resentment endangered his health, both body and soul. He knew those stories, told from the pulpit, about how wonderful it feels to forgive, what a burden it removes, how God can't forgive us unless we forgive others. He had gone through all the right motions, used the right words, sought no revenge, did kind and loving things. But the cold depths of pain were still untouched, unhealed. Sadly he concluded that he must be a very hard-hearted, unforgiving person, and therefore God would not forgive him either.

I fear I was not of much help to him. I listened, inwardly prayed, and at least did not give him the usual platitudes. But for me too the issues of forgiveness were almost impossibly difficult. It was not that I had experienced extreme trauma or wounding from others in my relatively happy life. But the few hurtful experiences I did have—bullying at school, disloyalty or neglect by a friend, resentment from a relative, rudeness from a coworker, a professional put-down, and so on—too often had become inner haunted houses for me. There I would angrily revisit the scenes of my wounding like a resentful ghost, clanking my chains of unfreedom. Parts of me felt trapped in these pockets of memory, these dungeons of pain. How impossible to let go and move on! Should such hurts be forgiven? What could possibly ever make up, compensate, for the injustice done, even if the perpetrator of my pain could be somehow forced to realize the injustice and apologize? Other parts of me would have *liked* to get out of those resentful dungeons, but no one told me *how*! Even if I outwardly forgave, how did I go about healing the hurt and angry feelings? Forgive "from your heart," Jesus said (Matthew 18:35). But how?

I experienced these difficulties for relatively light offenses. What were the feelings of people whose traumatic stories I increasingly heard? Their stories about betrayal and abuse were fathoms deeper than anything I had ever experienced. I have just read a news story of a five year-old boy, the only child of a loving single mother, killed by a drunk driver who already had four convictions of drunk driving and yet was still driving! The pastor at the funeral urged forgiveness. But how? Should such a thing *be* forgiven? And what could ever restore the child to that mother?

The stories of communal, generational devastation are the worst. What a challenge they present to any glib concept of forgiveness. In one of my classes, a woman student rose to say, "My parents come from a country in which there was an ethnic slaughter eighty years ago. No one was spared in their town, not tiny babies or weak old people. My parents were able to hide and escape, but they can't forget the smoke, the screams, the guns, the fire, the snarls of hatred. I can't forget either what they told me. How can one stop hating those monsters?" Yes, how?

Our counsel, even in our churches, has been appallingly superficial, insensitive, ignorant: "Get over it!" "That was then, this is now," "You should have put that behind you long ago," "Rise above it," "Put your mind on other things," "Look on the bright side," "Get on with your life," "Pray harder," "Don't you know that anger is unhealthy?" "Think of all the things *you've* done!" "Get rid of all those destructive feelings."

> We are called to forgive, but we are given no guidance in working with our feelings of anger, rage, disappointment and shame. . . . Unfortunately the popular understanding of the church's call to forgiveness has become a source of guilt for us rather than a way to personal freedom. . . . Not only hasn't the church given us a process through which we might achieve authentic forgiveness or a clear definition, but it has also been remiss in relaying the full message of Jesus in reference to his teachings on forgiveness and reconciliation.[1]

In this passage, Sandra Flaherty puts her finger on the crux of the anguished, usually unanswered question: What good does it do to say we forgive when underneath the words the dark, toxic river of unhealed pain and anger runs at deep levels, affecting our trust, the cells of our bodies, our feelings of safety and self-worth? In fact, the ways of *un*healthy forgiveness are constantly urged upon us.

I turned to the scriptures for guidance on this question. I knew, of course, about Jesus' reformation of the old law, which had enjoined, "You shall give life for life, eye for eye, tooth for tooth . . . burn for burn, wound for wound" (Exodus 21:23-25). Jesus challenged us instead, "You have heard that it was said, 'An eye for an eye. . . .' But I say to you, . . . if anyone strikes you on the right cheek, turn the other also" (Matthew 5:38-39). But this saying puzzled me also. Was Jesus really calling us to a life of victimhood, in which evil would have all its own way?

My questions increased when I realized that though we are challenged to return good for evil, to pray for those who hurt us, to love our enemies, Jesus uses the actual word *forgive* only when the wrongdoer has repented. Does that mean that though we may pray for those who hurt us, we forgive only when forgiveness is asked? I have not found a single passage in which Jesus specifically gives *personal* forgiveness to his enemies, except on the cross, and there he asks *God* to forgive.

And yet, Jesus had a great deal to forgive throughout his life. People in his hometown, Nazareth, tried to execute him; his own mother and brothers at one point (thinking he was deranged) tried to have him restrained; the authorities continually set traps for him and tried to lead him into self-recrimination; his own disciples sometimes tried to block his path; many towns refused to welcome him; the Romans had conquered his country. Judas betrayed him; Peter denied him; most of the disciples fled from the scene after his arrest. Yet never once does he say specifically, "I forgive you," but neither do I find any passage in which any of those who hurt him actually asked his forgiveness!

Nevertheless, obviously Jesus *did* forgive "from the heart." More deeply than mere words, he forgave, even when forgiveness was not asked. He healed the sick servant of the Roman centurion with no questions asked. One of his brothers James became one of his disciples. On the night in which he was betrayed he broke and shared the bread with *all* his disciples—knowing that one would betray him, another deny him, and that all would flee from him. Among his last words from the cross were arrangements for the care of his mother;

on resurrection night he gave the shalom (peace) to his disciples in hiding, called them "my brothers," and empowered them with the Holy Spirit; on the shores of Lake Tiberias he lovingly healed Peter of his deep shame at the denial. And what about Judas? Scripture does not tell us, but the ancient Christian creed asserts that after his death Jesus "descended into hell (Sheol)." Surely this meant he went to find Judas—as well as all of those trapped in despair who were willing to come to him.

Understanding, compassion, release, and healing flowed from Jesus' heart to all who had hurt him. How was this flow possible? Certainly Jesus did not repress his feelings. The scriptures tell us that sometimes he cried, became angry, showed exasperation, admitted even to loneliness.

Jesus was not in denial about the hurt and evil of the world. On the contrary he was totally clear-sighted and clear-spoken about what went on around him. He could read evil in the hearts of others as swiftly as he could discern their hidden potential for good.

Jesus certainly was not a passive victim! He resisted death several times. He did not allow anyone to silence him. All that he chose to do or not do, he *chose in freedom*. His choices rose from a center of strength, not weakness. Forgiveness for him, therefore, was not a surrender to the forces of evil. It was not a denial of reality. It was not a repression of feeling. It was not a condoning or excusing of an evil or abusive act. In no way whatever was it meant to be a victim stance.

What then is forgiveness in Jesus' teaching? I studied the whole Sermon on the Mount more carefully. It became clear that the central focus of that supreme teaching is *what is happening in our heart's core*. What we do outwardly springs from what we are thinking, feeling, choosing inwardly. If our root inner self is corrupt, hypocritical, infected with hatred, ill will, envy, then our outer actions also eventually will become lightless, corrupt, destructive.

Throughout the whole sermon, Jesus is talking about release from that which imprisons and corrupts our central heart—our heavy loads of resentment, fear, anxiety, shame, self-deception, cover-ups—and from the vicious cycles of revenge that continue to destroy both individuals and nations.

Forgiveness is a major release: a release from the prison and burden of the past. This release does not mean release from responsibility for what was done. Nor does release necessarily mean release from paying a penalty in this world. It means release from the chains of resentment and guilt that hold us back from entering God's freedom, the new beginning as a beloved child of God. It means release from the expectations and obligations of the past so that we and those who injured us may start anew.

This act of release does not depend on our own willpower. Jesus is telling us: Ground yourself in God, let your roots go down deep in God's renewing life, make God's realm (kingdom) your main center, let yourself be made anew, and what you most deeply need will flow toward you.

This renewal is not something that will happen sometime in the future. This realm of God's merciful empowerment already surrounds, embraces, us and springs up within us. Our ability to forgive flows from our increasing oneness with

21

that realm. Our forgiveness is not meant to be a victimhood to evil, a distant hope, or a rigid act of willpower. Ultimately forgiveness is not our power at all but God's power flowing toward us, in us, through us, like a mighty river. When we start the journey of forgiveness we *enter* that great current.

The journey of unfolding forgiveness is not a neat, tidy one. Nor does it necessarily move along the path in the order described in this book. We may find ourselves beginning at different places. We may need to return several times to certain stages. As we proceed, we may find we need to forgive a whole community rather than one person. Our journey may become one of *self-forgiveness* when we realize we ourselves have wounded others.

The word *journey* is misleading. I use it because forgiveness is so often considered a onetime act, whereas it is usually an ongoing, deepening process. But the word *process* sounds cold and mechanical. *Journey* sounds human, suggesting adventures and companions on the way, all of which is true of forgiveness. Nevertheless, the word *journey* itself *implies* that forgiveness is not true forgiveness until a goal is reached. It implies climbing a mountain and conquering a summit. But forgiveness is not a goal to be reached or a summit to be attained. The road itself *is* the goal! Once we have chosen to start this journey we are already within the great unfolding experience of forgiveness, though it may take us a long time to realize its fullness. A beautiful, ancient saying states: "In Christ, the there is here."

How is forgiveness possible? Forgiveness exists already— now and eternally. We do not create it; we enter it. As the deep meanings of forgiveness fold around us and unfold for us, we will experience the deepening and mingling of pain and power, sorrow and joy, clarity and ambiguity, adventure and security, in ways undreamed of.

CHAPTER TWO

Facing Our Hurt, Naming Our Need

~

Then he began to speak, and taught them, saying:
"Blessed are the poor in spirit, for theirs is the
kingdom of heaven."

—Matthew 5:2-3

What an unfortunate translation of this first mighty "Blessed"! It is enough to turn a seeker after healthy forgiveness away for life. "Poor in spirit"? What images these words evoke of spiritless, disempowered, washed-out victims.

Is this really what God wants of us? Is this what Jesus taught? Was Jesus himself like this? No, to all these questions. A more accurate translation from the root meanings of the Greek is "Blessed are those who recognize their total need of God."

Probably our journey of forgiveness will be impossible unless we realize we cannot do it alone. We are not the source of our healing. Truly the kingdom of God is within us as Jesus told us. But that kingdom is *God's* presence, and we need God's help to experience that inner glory.

As with any deep healing and release, the empowered mercy of God within and around us is ours to claim. We must face the facts: we are vulnerable (woundable); we have been hurt; we need to name our hurt and our deep needs as clearly and fully as we can. Little can change until we have faced where we actually are.

The basis of healthy forgiveness consists of asking these four questions honestly within the presence of God's love: (1) What happened? (2) Who is responsible? (3) How do I feel about what happened? (4) What is my need right now? Later we will ask another vital question: What are my choices at this time?

This clear seeing, clear naming can be incredibly scary. Victims of long-term abuse may find it much easier less painful to cover up the full reality of the hurt, to deny its devastating pain. It is so tempting to try to ignore what we feel, to make excuses, to rush to explain. Because this first step is so scary, Jesus endows those who take it with the full power of God's kingdom, that holy central source of strength and mercy.

We take our stance in the strength of this holy power when we can say first to ourselves and then to others: "Held by God's love, I ask God to help me name my hurt and need," then continue with examples such as:

- I was an abused, neglected child.
- My job situation is unjust and toxic.
- This is an abusive marriage.
- I am feeling pushed and bullied.
- I was betrayed and lied to.
- I was belittled and demeaned.

Or when facing a communal hurt:

- They enslaved and killed my people.
- My family has passed down pain and hurt for generations.
- This church destroys its servants and ministers.
- This is what happened to my country (racial group, ethnic group, religious group).

After an attempt to name our wounding as bluntly and clearly as possible, we need to add exactly what we feel about it and what we feel we need at this moment. For example: "I was criticized unjustly and humiliated at my job. At first I felt numb. Now I'm beginning to feel incredibly angry. I'm going to need some real help with this, God."

If we are naming a hurt we inflicted on another, we need God's help to be equally clear and direct: "Held within God's mercy, I ask God's help in naming what I did." For example:

- Yes, I did abuse my child.
- I bullied and pushed her.
- I demeaned his dignity.
- I broke faith, and lied to . . . .
- I neglected her when she needed me.
- My community did hurt that person (those people), and I share the responsibility.

Usually when naming an injury by another or by ourselves, we rush on to mitigations and explanations: "He hurt me because he was under such stress." "She spoke rudely and critically, but she wasn't feeling well." "I cut off that car because I've been cut off so often." "Yes, they abused and punished me severely as a child, but that was because they didn't know any better. It had been done to them."

The *becauses* come later, perhaps much later. They are important. But with this *first* step of facing our hurt or hurtfulness we need to stay with that special difficult focus of what actually happened, or we easily slip back into denial.

I know a woman who has endured injustice and demeaning acts and remarks at her workplace. She knows she has been treated humiliatingly, but the moment she names the truth of it, even to herself, she instantly adds, "Of course, it's a jungle out there. Everyone is under incredible stress fighting to keep their job." This statement undoubtedly is true, but at this moment she needs to look at what happened to *her* and be truthful about it; otherwise, her compassion and forgiveness will become blurred, befogged.

> Nothing is covered up that will not be uncovered, and nothing secret that will not become known. Therefore whatever you have said in the dark will be heard in the light, and what you have whispered behind closed doors will be proclaimed from the housetops. (Luke 12:2-3)

These tough words from Jesus were concerned with revealing cover-ups and hypocrisy, but they can also become our watchword for speaking the clear truth about what we formerly have denied or mitigated.

I believe that many of our liturgical confessions lead to ambiguity and even dishonesty about our real situation. Many of the things I am asked to confess from a printed communal confessional prayer are *not* necessarily my real sins and problems at that time. We need to encourage one another to look at what is really going on in our hearts and lives. Otherwise, confession loses its meaning and its power.

A liturgist might lead a group in this manner: "Within God's presence and holy mercy, let us each in our own heart ask if this week we have abused or demeaned the dignity of another," followed by a moment of silence. "Let us each ask within our heart if this week we have broken faith with someone who trusted us." The liturgist could continue in this vein.

What about confessions of communal guilt? They are needed, no question about that. But so often they are unclear and misleading: "*We* have persecuted the outcast . . . neglected the poor and hungry . . . wounded and demeaned other [racial groups, ethnic groups, minorities]" and so forth. This confession confuses the individual who may have spent much of his or her life working for justice, dignity, compassion for others; who has voted and petitioned for change on the political level; who has given of time, money, effort, thought for others.

If participants do not understand that a communal confession does not necessarily imply their *personal* guilt, again the confession will become meaningless, or the individuals involved will be overwhelmed with undeserved personal guilt feelings.

I believe all communal confessions should state clearly that the community is speaking *as a communal body* about its history of trespasses and debts: "As a community [church, nation, ethnic group] we confess that our communal choices and acts have often been unjust, wounding, demeaning, especially toward . . . ," naming the hurts for which the group as a body has been responsible. In this way individuals in this group who may be personally innocent of guilt may with honesty grieve over the wounding history of the group and share the sorrow and group responsibility.

Whether naming injury done to ourselves or done to another, it is an act of deep cleansing and power to name these incidents to ourselves and to God (and to others when appropriate) throughout the day and at the end of the day, no matter how trivial they may seem.

No, this is not the same as whining and self-pity. This is not the same as negative thinking. Whining, self-pity, and negative thinking rise out of our murky feelings. We fuss and whimper because we have not named our problem and our need with clarity. We experience a vague awareness that people are not nice, that we haven't received a fair deal. In the same way, chronic anger and irritability rise out of a basic underlying anger that has not been fully looked at. Chronic anxiety rises out of an underlying fear that has never been clearly, fully named.

Once we do name hurt and deep need, we move into another dimension altogether. We are no longer trapped. A window is open, and we are able to see where we are.

As we grow and deepen in our healing, we may need to return several times to this great first blessedness and name our problem more truthfully, because we will see the deeper dimensions of our pain. But at the beginning, all that is asked is to be as honest as we can within the enfolding strength of God. No matter how blunt and harsh our language sounds as we name our problem, we are already within the great unfolding act of forgiveness.

~

Suggested Meditation for Naming Your Hurt

Blessed are the poor in spirit,
for theirs is the kingdom of heaven (Matthew 5:3).

Let your body be comfortable. You can lie down, sit up, stand, or slowly walk. Breathe two or three slow, full breaths, as if breathing from the soles of the feet to the crown of the head. Then relax your breathing and let the breath come and go lightly and naturally.

Envision or think of God's presence in whatever way is most helpful to you. You might envision the presence of Jesus Christ; you might envision or think of a warm, soft light surrounding your body; strong, gentle hands holding you; wings sheltering you; a tree with great leafy branches against whose strength you lean; a powerful mountain holding you; or a green valley enclosing you.

If more helpful, you might inwardly say a word, a phrase, or a verse that helps you to feel God's nearness and empowered love, such as, *heart of love, healing light, hands of healing, breath of Spirit,* and so forth.

Remind yourself that you are in a safe place and that God's tender power is around you as you begin your journey of forgiveness.

Ask God's help to give a name to your hurt, your injury— as definite a name as possible. If naming your hurt feels frightening, ask the living Christ to name it for you. Or you can inwardly say it with God, together in your heart.

Name the hurt and name the persons involved, whether it is something that happened in the past or something going on right now, whether it is a serious trauma or a trivial injury. Be as clear as you can, with God strengthening you, to put in words what you feel is the real situation.

You and God look at this together. Decide if you are ready to start your forgiving, releasing process. Remember that the living Jesus Christ not only is beside you on this journey, but also has gone ahead to prepare the way for you.

If you have injured another and are seeking forgiveness for yourself, go through the same steps of bodily relaxation, claiming the presence of God in whatever way is most vivid and helpful for you, whether by envisioning or by saying words inwardly.

Know that you too are surrounded by God's merciful strength as you ask for help in naming as exactly as possible in words the wound you inflicted on another person.

Remind yourself that the living Christ walks beside you, every step, and also goes ahead to prepare the way.

Whether you are the wounded or the wounder, give thanks that you are being helped to name the hurt clearly.

Try also to put in inner words exactly what you feel you need right now. Be as blunt and direct as possible. God understands your heart and does not condemn either what you feel or how you say it.

Bring your attention back to your body. Does any special part of your body at this moment seem to need a gentle touch of comfort and reassurance? Lay your hand upon this bodily part very gently, or ask the present Christ to lay hands upon it.

Breathe deeply two or three times, then relax your breath. Give a gentle massage to your face and hands and wrists. Stretch. Know that God remains with you even as you bring your meditation to an end.

Slowly make a reentry into your daily life.

CHAPTER THREE

Making Sacred Space for Pain, Grief, and Anger

> *Blessed are those who mourn,*
> *for they will be comforted.*
>
> —Matthew 5:4

*L*uke's translation says more bluntly, "Blessed are those who cry." One of the greatest blocks to healthy forgiveness is trying to push too quickly past our emotional pain when we have been hurt.

If it is scary to name our hurt clearly, it is painful to let ourselves really feel the suffering from a past or present wound. To admit and feel emotional pain is to admit that we are not the invulnerable person we thought we were. We are woundable. Other people have the power to hurt us. To admit and feel this hurts us all over again.

Also we fear seeming weak and self-pitying to others. We may feel ashamed that we have not been able to put the pain behind us. We wonder if thinking about it, feeling our feelings, will make the pain worse or if we will get trapped in a prison of brooding. We worry lest our negative emotions endanger our health.

People around us, either because they want to help us or because they feel uncomfortable with our pain, may be telling us to hurry up and get over it. They urge us to look on the bright side and allow only positive feelings. This advice may be urged on us with the best intentions. Countless retreat leaders tell their retreatants to leave all their troubles and worries at the door when they come in. They lead participants in bodily exercises to shake out all negativity, teach them breathing routines to exhale all sorrow and anger. I know no quicker route to *un*healthy forgiveness!

Making sacred space for genuine mourning over our wounds is essential within the journey of healthy forgiveness. Genuine mourning involves many feelings, including anger and sorrow, which are closely intertwined. One is often a disguise for the other. For example, if sorrow has settled into a long depression, we may have neglected to look at the genuine anger we are feeling. Or, if our anger grows out of hand and we unload it inappropriately on those around us, perhaps it is because we have not let ourselves cry. For some of us, it feels safer and easier to rage than to cry. Rage is often our masked tears.

If a gray fog of sadness has settled over our lives it may mean that we have not let ourselves express active *sorrow*. Active sorrow is a feeling clearly linked to the source of grief.

Sadness, on the other hand, is a passive condition that quickly becomes pervasive if we do not name and grieve for our true sorrow.

Mourning includes more than anger and sorrow. Mourning can include a feeling of vulnerability after we have been hurt. We feel like a target. Now that such a hurt has happened, we wonder if it will happen again. We feel unprotected in a hurtful, dangerous world, wondering whom we can trust.

Shame is often a response to being wounded, though this feeling is often overlooked. We may feel humiliated, somehow rendered unclean and unworthy when we have been abused. It is a well-documented fact that victims of abuse (whether children, spouses, the elderly, employees, church members) often do not name or report abuse because they feel shame and embarrassment that such a thing has happened to them. They may feel they have brought it on themselves and are unworthy of help. They may even feel shame on behalf of the abuser!

Healthy forgiveness is usually impossible if these feelings are pushed past too quickly in the name of forgiveness. Such feelings do not go away until they are healed. If we thrust feelings down out of our conscious awareness, they can smolder for years in our deep subconscious selves, damaging the very cells of our bodies.

Some years ago I visited a church that was hundreds of years old. Our guide pointed out a crusted, blackened area in one of the old oak ceiling beams: "A slow fire began there," he told us, "deep inside that old wood. It smoldered unseen for many months, spreading slowly, creeping through the wood until it began to show on the outside.

Then when it reached the air, it began to flame. We could hardly save the roof in time!"

We Christians are taught to be suspicious of anger, and many of us have felt that anger has no place within forgiveness. But anger serves as a warning signal that we sense a threat to something of value to us. Dennis, Sheila, and Matthew Linn tell us:

> The gift of anger is that it locates our wound, helps us defend ourselves and energizes us to correct what needs correction. . . . Lingering anger usually indicates we moved too quickly through the forgiveness process . . . . Anger at abuse and injustice is an expression of our integrity and our dignity as human beings.[1]

I have also learned to my surprise that anger can be part of the inner vitality that heals us. Dr. Rachel Remen, in her struggle against chronic illness, discovered the uses of anger with amazed insight one day: "Shocked, I recognized the connection between my anger and my will to live. My anger was my will to live turned inside out. . . . My anger had helped me to survive, to resist my disease."[2]

What Dr. Remen discovered in her illness, we can discover also in our experiences of being abused. Our anger was part of our strength, our will to live and keep going, and thus needs to be honored and to be heard.

As with the distinction between active sorrow and passive sadness, there is a difference between active, healthy anger directed at something or someone and a generalized, pervasive rage and irritability. The latter reflects anger that has become infected *because* we have not looked for the source, named it, and allowed ourselves to feel it in its early, healthy stages.

Will we get stuck at this early stage of anger? Will we be so intoxicated with the energy of legitimate anger that we become addicted to this energy? Addiction can develop if our healing journey stops there, but if we let our healing deepen, anger assumes a different form. Dr. Remen reflects on the change:

> I still get angry sometimes but in ordinary ways. My anger does not begin to compare to the rage that was my life companion for all those years. That rage served me well. It defended my integrity. It said no to the limitations of my disease, but something else would be required to say yes to my life.[3]

What about trivial hurts? Working through feelings at depth may be necessary for victims of long, severe abuse and injustice, but is it necessary for everyday types of injury, such as being barked at rudely by a clerk or client, being excluded from a party, being cut off by a car on the highway, and so forth?

A process of healing and forgiving is necessary even for slight offenses, though it may take only minutes instead of days and years. Continually shrugging off small, painful abuses and injuries as if they do not matter or as if *we* do not really matter is not healthy. If we become entrenched in the dangerous mind-set that Christians ought to go through the day as submissive victims, a dangerous buildup of unfaced anger can suddenly explode all over innocent bystanders.

Also we need to ask ourselves what we mean by *trivial*. Why does it sometimes take longer to forgive an apparently slight offense than a far more serious injury?

"Why do I keep brooding about the fact that she didn't invite me to her open house?" a woman once asked me. As we talked, it occurred to us that she, without realizing it, associated this trivial neglect with childhood years when she felt different from others at school and was often left out. She had gone on, building up confidence in her professional work, putting those painful years of rejection at school behind her to the point where she had almost forgotten it. But the suffering little girl inside her had not forgotten, and a small incident had opened up years of neglected, uncleansed, unhealed pain. Someone described this kind of experience powerfully to me just the other day: "We step into what we think is a child's wading pool and find it to be a deep, dark lake!"

How do we make a sacred, safe space for our mourning? We may need an actual temporary separation from the injuring person or situation in order to experience healing in safety. Certainly serious abuse—in our home, our workplace, our church, our friendships—necessitates our leaving that house, job, church, friend, at least for a while, so we can let ourselves feel our feelings and begin to make decisions and choices. We are not safe to heal and make changes if we remain in the same critically abusive environment. Jesus had to walk away from his hometown, Nazareth, when people there tried to stop his ministry with physical violence (see Luke 4:16-30).

In situations that are not so critical, we may well need a time of emotional distancing. We may need to stop meeting or talking with the other person for a while, taking the space and time we need before we interact again.

Even when dealing with hurts that are truly trivial, it is

wise to create an inner safe space, an inner distancing, if only for a few moments to face what has happened and what we feel about it. We can go into another room, take a walk, gaze at a tree or plant, take a few breaths at an open window, close our eyes for a few minutes.

For the more serious hurts we need to make sacred space by contacting trusted friends or a good therapist who will help guide us safely through the pain of experiencing our feelings more fully. Probably we will not be able to do this all in one session. We may need to return repeatedly to such sharing, allowing awareness of our true feelings to deepen gradually.

It is important to be honest with God in prayer or in a journal, saying what we really do feel without "stained-glass" language. God already knows what we feel and understands. Leaf through the psalms. Many of them are filled with anger, fear, sorrow, shame—even anger at God—shared openly with God. An example is Psalm 139—an almost unsurpassed song of love and trust in God's closeness:

> Where can I go from your spirit?
> Or where can I flee from your presence?
> If I ascend to heaven, you are there;
> if I make my bed in Sheol [hell], you are there.
> If I take the wings of the morning...
> even there your shall hand lead me,
> and your right hand shall hold me fast. (verses 7-10)

In the midst of this loving, trustful prayer, the tone changes suddenly, radically. The psalmist becomes aware of rage and hatred rising in him:

O that you would kill the wicked, O God . . . .
I hate them with perfect hatred;
    I count them my enemies. (verses 19, 22)

He has felt safe expressing his rage before God, knowing God understands. Significantly he concludes his prayer by asking God to cleanse his heart:

Search me, O God, and know my heart . . .
See if there is any wicked [hurtful] way in me,
    and lead me in the way everlasting. (verses 23-24)

We can picture our anger, sorrow, and shame flying like arrows into the sun or flying like wounded birds directly into God's heart, where God will hold them with strong compassion. Ask God for your own inner picture of a special place where you can let yourself feel your feelings and receive the comfort. You may want to draw it, paint it, mold it, dance it. You may want to make a nest on the floor with pillows and crawl into it for a while.

Scripture speaks of many such safe, sacred places: green pastures, still waters, strong tables of rock, "in the presence of my enemies" (Psalm 23), mountains, God's sheltering wings, God's strong hands, God's shield around us.

Jesus gives us a poignant picture of a safe, healing place in his story of a poor man Lazarus and the rich man who let Lazarus starve and die on his doorstep (Luke 16:19-31). When both men die, Lazarus is taken to shelter in "Abraham's bosom" (the older translation) where he is healed and comforted. The rich man, now burning in the cleansing flames of remorse, sees Lazarus sheltered in Abraham's bosom (which I think is the same as the heart of God in this story). He asks Abraham to send Lazarus to cool him with water; in other words, to minister to him. Abraham calls him "my child," for God still loves us and calls us child even when we are in a hell of our own making. Abraham explains, however, that it is now the time for Lazarus to be comforted and that a great gulf separates Lazarus from his former abuser.

After serious abuse, we do indeed need a feeling of a gulf, a real separation from the abuser. We need to feel safe while we heal. We need that time and space for ourselves. Above all we need that place in God's heart (however we experience it) where we will be comforted.

"Right now I don't want to help my brother in any way," a woman minister once said to me. "I don't want to pray for him. He used and abused me for years, and I don't want any part of me used for him or by him again. At least, that's the way I feel now." I honored her honesty. She needed more time to feel safe.

Will Lazarus someday wish to bring water to his abuser? I believe so. But this readiness must never be pushed or hurried. To rush ourselves or another into immediate ministry to the abuser is abuse all over again!

Finding a safe place to feel our feeling is not an escape or a running away from reality. Being in a safe place allows time for an inner drawing together, a form of deep centering, putting roots down in God's vast love. This time allows emotional and spiritual healing while enclosed by God's protection, God's comfort.

Comfort. It is a powerful word, and it means many things. Certainly it implies shelter, enfoldment, supportive closeness, but it means even more. A woman who worked through the hurt of spousal abuse told me: "When I first felt the comfort of God, it was like being held, rocked in someone's arms. Sometimes I felt it was like the way I used to be rocked in my grandmother's lap in her rocking chair. But then there was more to it. I felt new strength pouring into me, a strange power and hopefulness. I hadn't felt either power or hope for so long."

The night before his death Jesus promised to send his Holy Spirit to the disciples. In Greek, the Holy Spirit is called the Paraclete, which has been variously translated as the Comforter, the Counselor, the Advocate, but the basic meaning of Paraclete is "the one who stands by you and calls you forth." A true comforter does exactly that for us: stands by us in our pain and problem as long as we need that steadfast presence, but does not let us get stuck in a prison of pain indefinitely. Eventually we are healed and strengthened to the point where we move forward into new life, new choices, and growing.

I am deeply moved by this witness of a cult abuse survivor who describes the presence and action of the Comforter in her own life and that of others:

> Every ritual abuse survivor has an inner part that somehow stayed connected to life even in the midst of torture and death. This part . . . though buried deep inside, never lost a sense of the spiritual, the holy. . . . It nurtured life within us and throughout our abuse and our remembering. . . . It may have many names: the strong one, the keeper of the spirit, the healer, the mystic, the grandparent, the wise one. . . . This strong one within has a natural longing for life and healing. It is wise beyond years. It knows about pain and healing

and spirit. . . . It guides us in the healing journey if we give it room to do so.[4]

Is the mourning process appropriate if *we* have been the abuser, the wounder? Never more so! No mourning is deeper than that which follows our honest naming of the hurt we have inflicted. We will need a safe space to honor this grieving. We will experience the active sorrow for inflicting injury and our inability to undo the past. We will hurt for the pain of the other. We will feel shock and shame at our capacity for injuring someone else. We will feel anger at ourselves and maybe anger at God who permitted our act. We may feel genuine fear that we may act this way again.

All these feelings and more fed the flame that the rich man in Jesus' parable was experiencing. He was appalled at his hard-heartedness toward Lazarus. He wished he could go back and change things. He longed to share with his brothers still alive on earth what he had learned.

What were Paul's feelings as he looked back through the years to the time when he was Saul and stood watching with approval as a crowd hideously stoned Stephen to death? How did he feel as he remembered the days when he set his furious force to hunting down Christians?

> . . . with your remembered faces,
>   Dear men and women, who I sought and slew!
> Ah when we mingle in the heavenly places
>   How will I weep to Stephen and to you!
> . . . .
> Also I ask, but ever from the praying
>   Shrinks my soul backward, eager and afraid,

Point me the sum and shame of my betraying,
 Show me, o Love, the wounds which I have made!

Yes, thou forgivest, but with all forgiving
 Canst not renew mine innocence again:
Make thou, o Christ, a dying of my living,
 Purge from the sin but never from the pain![5]

This poem, *Saint Paul*, written over a century ago, expresses what Paul must have felt. But the Holy Spirit, the Paraclete, the Comforter, stood by him and called him forth. His sorrow was not to lead to a dead end. God called him (and us) to a new creation.

I believe also that the rich man of Jesus' parable had not reached a dead end. He was burning with remorse in Sheol. He felt sorrow. He wanted to help his brothers. God through Abraham called him still "my child." The great gulf was there for the safety, comfort, and healing of Lazarus, but in God's heart there is no gulf. In our self-made hells, whether in this life or the next, God still calls us "my child," and the Holy Spirit stands next to us, calling us forth.

We need to remember that even as new persons in a new creation, we will still feel some sorrow whether we are the injured or the injurer. Harm has been done, and the bodily or emotional damage in this life may be permanent. This mature, genuine sorrow should not be confused with non-forgiveness either of others or ourselves. This sorrow is the aching of old scar tissue. Jesus' wounds on his risen body after Easter had become sources and signs of transformation and healing for others. Nevertheless, they were still wound marks. Pain and sorrow are never wasted when given into

God's hands, and their transformation is far beyond our imaginings. But in this life, we will experience a poignancy, a regret that harm was done when our actions could have been different. This poignancy is a valid, healthy part of our journey of release.

The deepest comfort in our mourning is to know that God not only has compassion but actually feels our suffering with us. Jesus tells us that not even a tiny sparrow will fall to the ground "apart from your Father" (Matthew 10:29). To me this means that God's heart so enfolds and unites with the sparrow (and with us) that the suffering of the tiny creature is shared, felt by that supreme heart. The creature's suffering resounds through God's whole being.

I'll never forget a story I heard from a woman at a retreat some years ago. It has become for me a profound metaphor of God's incarnation in Jesus and also of God's sharing our pain right now, the pain of the world as well as the pain of each one of us.

The woman told us that she had brought home from the animal shelter a young dog abused by former owners. The dog was especially terrified by water. Perhaps someone had tried to drown him. Eventually, of course, he had to be washed thoroughly, especially after running in thickets, picking up insects, and bleeding from thorns. When she put the dog into the tub of water, he screamed, struggled, and scratched her in his terror. Her whole heart hurt for him. She could do only one thing. She climbed into the dirty, bloody bathwater with him. Some of the blood in the water came from her own scratches. There she sat close to him, holding him in her arms, stroking him until his panic subsided. Then, still in the bathwater with him, she began to cleanse him—very gently.

This is the story of God's heart, and these are the acts of God's hands right now as we move through our journey of mourning.

~

Suggested Meditation for Feeling the Pain of Our Wound

Blessed are those who mourn,
for they will be comforted (Matthew 5:4).

Move through this meditation with great gentleness toward yourself. If your feeling of pain increases to a point that seems threatening, move out of the meditation, pray in some other way, leave the room and share your feeling with someone you trust. You might want someone with you during this whole meditation.

You may wish to try different sections of this meditation at different times. You can leave the meditation and return to it as often as you need to.

Relax your body in whatever way feels most comfortable. Breathe a few slow, deep breaths; then relax your breathing to a gentle, normal rhythm.

Claim the presence of God, the love of God through Jesus Christ who is beside you, on this journey with you. God already has strengthened you to name your hurt in clear words. Name it again. Rest a few moments.

When you feel ready, ask God to strengthen you in your mourning. This is a necessary step in healing and forgiveness, even for trivial hurts. What are you feeling now as you look at what has hurt you? Are you angry? How does your anger feel in your body? Like a great wave crashing on the shore? a flight of arrows shooting into the sky? a volcano erupting lava? a bolt of lightning and crashing thunder? an inner screaming?

You may need to express your anger bodily by clenching your fists and jaw, pounding a pillow, tearing up a sheet of paper, shaking fists in the air.

You may want to draw your anger with vivid colors—the shape and hue of your anger. You may wish to dance it, expressing your feeling with your whole body. God's presence surrounds you and you are safe. It is safe to show your anger to God if you need to. Write a letter to God—or draw it, dance it, or just say it.

Are you feeling sadness, grief? Try to let your sadness become an active act of sorrow. Cry if you want. Picture yourself in a heavy rain or under a weeping waterfall. Cover your face and rock back and forth if that feels like what you need.

You may want to draw your feeling of sorrow, sculpt it, or express it with bodily movements. Go outdoors and pick up objects from nature that reflect the way you feel: a withered leaf, a battered rock; a dead butterfly, a dry stick, a torn flower. Arrange what you have found on a surface.

Whatever feeling you have as you mourn your hurt, be as spontaneous as possible. Know that God understands what you feel and that you have a right to express your feeling.

If you are mourning an injury you have done to another, remind yourself that your feeling is a necessary step in healing. *Never do injury to yourself as recompense in your self-anger.* That is not acceptable. Cling to the presence of the living Jesus and share your sorrow. This is the way Saint Peter and Saing Paul felt after their wounding acts. Grieving is necessary, and God will help you through it. God also is offering healing and a new life. Weep your sorrow and shame, but do not harm yourself. You belong to God.

Picture or just think of the person you have hurt being held and comforted by God. Pray that this comforting may bring a deep healing to that person.

As you bring this stage of your meditation to a close, come very gently forth from your experience of mourning. Take several minutes to become aware of your body. Your body has carried much of the weight and burden of unexpressed anger and sorrow. Do any bodily parts need to be touched with healing touch? the heart area? abdomen? eyes? jaw muscles? Touch these parts with extreme gentleness. Inwardly speak to your body and tell it that it does not need to carry the burden alone anymore, that it can release the heaviness and congestion.

Ask God to carry your pain to God's heart where it will be held and comforted. Can you make a picture of this? Or put it into words?

Stretch, yawn fully, massage hands, wrists, and face. Give thanks to God who is still with you. Begin to reenter your daily life.

Chapter Four

Away from Force into God's Gentle Power

~

Blessed are the meek,
for they will inherit the earth.
—Matthew 5:5

$\mathcal{M}$y student, an alert and intelligent middle-aged man, sat in my office at the theological school, telling me about an occurrence in a class earlier in the day. He had shared with the class an art project that he had worked on all semester. "They tore it to pieces with their comments," he told me in a level voice. "The women students especially thought it was demeaning, and they expressed a lot of criticism, even outrage."

"How do you feel about this?" I asked him. "Bitter? I know you worked hard on it for a long time and gave it your best. It must have been very hurtful."

51

"Yes," he answered, "it did hurt somewhat, and I was startled by their reaction. But then I realized they needed to say what they felt. I tried to listen to them. What they said seemed to rise out of a lot of their pain. I tried to see it from their point of view, and I think it's helped me in some ways in my artwork."

I looked at him with a feeling akin to awe. I knew how I would have reacted if a whole class had attacked my term project! Two thoughts flashed through my mind: This is an unusual person, and, So *that's* what the Bible really means by *meek*.

This student did not behave in a way we usually think of when we hear the word *meek*. He was not self-effacing, passive, or submissive. He knew his worth, and he knew that his intentions had been good. But he listened, he was open to change, and he responded to this experience out of an inner power rather than force.

Listening to God, to others, to ourselves; being willing to learn and to change; responding out of God's gentle power rather than out of defensiveness or aggression—these are the meanings of meekness. Jesus, so often described as "meek and mild," appears in scripture as one who makes no weak surrender to unrighteousness. Scripture shows his strength, his courage, the firmness of his stand. We see his fierce anger against child abuse (see Matthew 18:5-6), against mercilessness, hypocrisy, and the stony-hearted neglect of the poor and the powerless. He was a man of laughter and joy and celebration as well as pain. He had power to attract, lead, and transform others. Vast healing power poured forth from him. Though sometimes angry, he was never arrogant. Apparently this portrayal represents the biblical meaning of meekness!

Away from Force into God's Gentle Power

I did some research on the root meanings of the word *humble*, a synonym for meek. That too is a word of uncomfortable associations. It sounds like a self-effacing crawling, but one of its original meanings from the Greek was "to walk without strutting"!

Jesus has promised those who are firm without arrogance, those who are eager to learn and grow, those who are willing to change and willing to be helped, those who respond to others out of God's gentle strength rather than mere force, that they will "inherit the earth."

Jesus must have been thinking of Psalm 37, which uses "inherit the land" five times in describing those who are gentle, strong, expectant. (*Land* and *earth* are used interchangeably.)

The whole psalm centers around the true biblical meaning of meekness:

Do not fret because of the wicked. . . .
   Trust in the Lord, and do good. . . .
Commit your way to the Lord. . . .
Do not fret—it leads only to evil. . . .
Those who wait for the Lord shall inherit the land.
(verses 1, 3, 5, 8, 9)

We find no surrender to evil here. These words do not summon us to weak submission and powerlessness but to a different kind of power. This new power neither invades nor defends, yet it is the toughest, most enduring and transforming energy in the world—an empowered vulnerability that is not victimhood.

What about the guidance to turn the other cheek when struck (Matthew 5:39)? Doesn't this passage seem to imply total submission to unjust injury? Quite the contrary, according to Walter Wink in his masterful trilogy on the Christian encounter with evil.

Wink reminds us that the verse speaks specifically of being struck on the *right* cheek. The significance of this designation would have been understood instantly by those who heard Jesus. In the cultures of the East, the right hand was the clean, honored hand used for eating, greeting friends, or fighting with an enemy you considered your worthy equal. The left hand was used for unclean tasks, including striking an inferior.

The only way to hit someone on the right cheek was either by using the left, unclean, hand (an insult) or the *back* of the right hand, also a sign of contempt. Therefore, to turn the other cheek, the left one in this case, challenged the one who had struck to use the palm of the right hand. This gesture was a quiet, nonviolent but powerful way to remind one's insulter of one's dignity and equality in the face of the deliberate insult.

> This action robs the oppressor of the power to humiliate. The person who turns the other cheek is saying, in effect, "Try again. Your first blow failed to achieve its intended effect. I deny you the power to humiliate me." . . . Gandhi taught, "the first principle of nonviolent action is that of non-cooperation with everything humiliating."[1]

Wink goes on to clarify the real implications in some of the other passages in the same scripture, such as giving up one's cloak if the coat has been taken and going the second mile. We need to understand these examples in the context of their time and particular culture, and then we try to apply the basic meaning to our daily lives today.

How can we turn the other cheek, responding out of power rather than force in ordinary encounters with those who may be opposing us? If someone makes an insulting remark we usually react in one of four ways: (1) instantly retaliating, returning insult for insult; (2) launching into defensive explanations; (3) falling silent and brooding; or (4) deflecting the hurt by making a joke out of it. But if we can take a moment to breathe slowly and deeply and then respond from God's power, we can look the offender in the face and say quietly and firmly, "I wonder if you really meant that in the way it sounded. If so, it's time we talk about the real issues."

If someone turns aside a serious conversation with flippant, inappropriate remarks, instead of giving a weak laugh or responding irritably, we can turn the other cheek of empowered dignity, turn our full attention to the joker and say thoughtfully, "Is there something about this conversation that makes you uncomfortable? Let's look at this together."

If at our workplace or at home someone gives a sharp, cutting criticism, we can meet it directly, saying, "The way you are saying this is hurtful, but I'm trying to hear the real gist of your criticism. I think I might learn something from your point if we can talk about it in another way."

This way of responding (and I have a long way to go learning it!) rises from our own sense of worth, combined with willingness to learn and grow. It is not submission, nor is it aggression or defensiveness.

Of course, in situations of serious abuse, we will need to establish firmer limits and make harder choices, as Jesus did when he left Nazareth rather than let himself be killed. Setting such limits differs from retaliation, insult for insult.

Jesus is quoted as saying, "Do not resist an evildoer" (Matthew 5:39). The better translation is this: "Do not use evil methods against evildoers." If we become abusive to our abusers, if we lie to those who have lied to us, if we offer rudeness and arrogance against the rudely arrogant, we take on the very nature of our abusers and become like them. We also become increasingly locked into the deep and dreadful cycles of vengeful feuding that has destroyed (whether emotionally or physically) families, communities, and nations for centuries.

I am spending a lot of time with this point because learning how to encounter our opponents is vitally important in our journey of forgiveness. We must seek a way other than reacting with force at one extreme or submission at the other. Jesus points us to the open, gentle power that can change our heart.

I was surprised when I suddenly realized that we are to become meek to ourselves! When we have negative, inappropriate urges and thoughts, when we make mistakes, when we fail and fall short of our self-expectations, we tend to submit sadly to our dark side with a "we're-all-human" attitude, to blot it out with self-denial, or to become emotionally violent with merciless self-contempt and anger.

Another way is offered to us. We can learn to turn with both openness and power to our disconcerting and troubling thoughts and impulses, saying to them: What are you really trying to tell me? From what need or hurt do you come? Is God trying to tell me something through you? What can I learn from you about my needs and inner healing?

This different form of response is not "giving in." Giving in shows no respect either to the other or to ourselves. Instead it is a sincere listening with a willingness to learn. If we do not learn to respect and to hear what our inner needs are trying to tell us, we probably will not be able to listen at depth to what others are trying to say. Thus our growing is blocked. If we respond to our own selves with power rather than force, increasingly we will respond to others this way.

Some outer force is still needed. We need police, law enforcement, national defense. In this world we still have to defend ourselves physically sometimes. Jesus allowed his disciples to bring swords into the Garden of Gethsemane on the night he was arrested (see Luke 22:36-38). He did not allow them to use their swords to defend him, and he rebuked Peter when Peter tried to fight for him. Jesus had chosen another way and was drawing upon God's power only, but he allowed the disciples to have the means to defend themselves.

The immune system is our own body's constant alertness, expelling or destroying bacteria, viruses, toxic substances, with *force.* This slowly evolving world still needs some force. Many scripture passages promise us that it will not always be this way. Scripture tells us that as individuals and communities we can begin to open ourselves to the deep power within ourselves, a radiating light of transformation that changes us from the heart rather than forcing outward compliance.

This gentle power of inner transformation already works in the world—in us, among us, through us. We can see the power of inner transformation in the way yeast quietly leavens bread dough, in the way living plants thrust through the soil. Someday this power for transformation will become the strength of the whole world.

In my own lifetime I have seen incredible changes in the world. Yes, we do have terrible problems and perplexities. Yes, evil is very much alive and reaches us in new, insidious ways. As from the beginning of recorded history, there are still wars, devastations, destructions. But I do not believe that we are to wait, expecting the worst, counting on a wrathful God to end everything in a single ruinous blow. Jesus told us he is with us forever, among us now, working with us, his vast kingdom of transforming love spreading quietly but ever more deeply.

We can see changes wrought by Jesus' love if we do not allow ourselves to be terrorized by predictors of doom. There was no United Nations when I was a child; war was still glorified; lynchings were still common; domestic abuse was denied and covered up; there was little equality or justice for women in politics, ministry, business, academia, medicine; there were few interracial schools. (My excellent "liberal" high school in Michigan had only one black student out of three hundred students in the six years I was there.) There was little if any concern over pollution of air, earth, and water. The lakes and rivers were almost dead with toxic wastes. If anyone fought for whales, seals, or redwood trees, I never heard of them. There was no welfare program.

At that time, nations and churches did not ask one another's forgiveness, ever. There was little awareness or compassion for political and natural disasters in other lands. There was no feeling of this being *one* world.

There is a change in spite of our many problems. We are

beginning to listen to one another. We are admitting need for changes. In an almost unbelievable way concern and compassion for the suffering have deepened. Christ is at work among us, just as he promised. The meek are beginning to be heard. In my lifetime there has been a Gandhi, a Martin Luther King, a Mother Teresa, a Nelson Mandela, and each has been heard and honored around the world.

> See, the Lord God comes with might,
>   and his arm rules for him. . . .
> He will feed his flock like a shepherd;
>   he will gather the lambs in his arms.
> (Isaiah 40:10-11)

Could there be a more vivid picture of the power that is gentle and the gentleness that is powerful! *God has forever renounced force over us!*

As we learn to be empowered in our gentleness, open to God, one another, ourselves, by our very existence we expand the realm of the meek, who have been promised the whole earth. And even now, even before the realm of the open, the gentle, the expectant, covers the earth, as each of us individually opens to and enters into God's gentle power, we already have inherited the earth of God's vision. We already are rooted and grounded in the world of God's will.

~

Suggested Meditation on Moving Away from Force into God's Power

Blessed are the meek,
for they will inherit the earth (Matthew 5:5).

Rest your body, breathe deeply two or three times, then breathe with light, normal breath.

Think of or picture God's closeness in whatever way feels best for you.

You are at a point in the journey of forgiveness where God opens doors to new growing, new possibilities, new expectancy.

If inner envisioning is natural to you, you might picture a door opening and the living Christ (in whatever form) entering, sitting next to you, and asking, "Are you ready for the next step?" Give an honest answer.

If you feel ready, ask yourself, What do I feel is taking place within me at this stage of my forgiveness journey? Take a few moments of silence. Notice if a word, phrase, an inner picture, or symbol comes especially into your consciousness. You may wish to write it down or draw what you sense.

If you feel ready to move on, ask God's help to distinguish clearly the difference between the stances of force and defensiveness as contrasted with the realm of God's gentle power.

Whether you have been hurt by another or have hurt another, ask yourself, What was a situation in which I tried to use force? Did I retaliate with name-calling? Did I use some form of emotional pushing or battering? Did I threaten either overtly or subtly? Did I manipulate? Did I interrupt or refuse to listen? Did I show cold contempt?

What are my bodily signals when I am about to use force on another or myself: clenched jaw, clenched fist, curling toes, burning behind the eyes, pounding heart, sharp jagged breathing? Can I learn to identify these signals in the early stages? How did these forcible methods affect me after the incident?

What was a situation in which I was defensive? Did I stiffen up and refuse to listen? Was I so busy with explanations that I could not hear either God or the other person? Did I withdraw in pride and shame and put myself behind a wall so thick no one could reach me? What were my bodily signals? Did I want to mask my face? Did my muscles get still and rigid? Did I forget to breathe slowly and deeply? Did my shoulders hunch over, compressing my heart and lungs?

How would the situation have been different if I had felt God's power around me, if I had leaned on that power, slowly and deeply breathed in that power, let it well up within me like a fountain of fresh water?

How would my body have felt? Would I have been able to look at what was happening and listen to what was said? What if I had taken a short space of silence to ask God how to respond?

What if I could have taken a moment to ask myself, What am I learning at this moment? How can I be open without being submissive?

Take a few moments for silent reflection. You might wish to draw, paint, write, or express with your body how you feel the difference between force, defense, and God's power. Let your bodily responses begin to learn the difference.

Now think of some situation ahead of you in which you may be in a difficult encounter with another. Ask the living Christ to go ahead of you to prepare that place for you, so that when you get there, in time you will feel the welcome and the special strength God gives. Think of yourself or envision yourself surrounded with God's light, breathing God's breath, giving yourself a space for listening, reflecting, then acting out of that center of inner strength rather than *re*acting.

Give thanks to God that a deep change already is working within you. God's gentle, radical power is re-creating you.

Yawn, stretch, give a light massage to your face, hands, and wrists, and reenter your daily life.

CHAPTER FIVE

Release to New Healing Choices

~~~

Blessed are those who hunger and thirst for righteousness,
for they will be filled.
—Matthew 5:6

*M*aking clear, strong choices may be the hardest part of forgiveness for many people. As we approach the beatitude after this one, which blesses the merciful, it is necessary to claim what seems like the hardness of this fourth blessedness, the search for righteousness and justice.

Mercy was never meant to negate justice; mercy unfolds *within* the context of righteousness. Perhaps a better way of putting it is that justice is the grounding rod of mercy.

It *is* merciful to be concerned for what is right for the wounder as well as the wounded. If we submit powerlessly to an abuser, we are doing serious harm to the abuser who becomes confirmed and increasingly trapped in his or her own toxic personality, eventually destroying the health and integrity of the personality. The greatest wrong we can do an abuser is to allow that person to invade, trespass, violate the freedom and healthy boundaries of another.

Recently I talked with a woman who has lived with her invasive mother for years. "She reads my letters; she listens in on phone conversations; she insists I include her in all my outings with friends; she tells me what I ought to wear and when I should return home. She gets desperately hurt and refuses to speak to me when I point out that I'm in my thirties and need private space in my life. But I don't feel I can move out. She's an invalid and is totally impractical in finances and daily life and really needs someone to care for her. No, it's not dementia or senility. She has been this way as far back as I can remember. She acted the same way with my father. Is God telling me to be more patient and acquiescent?"

As we sat together in silence, reflecting, I remembered what a minister had recently shared with me. "Someone gave me a surprising and powerful insight the other day," I told the woman. "He pointed out that to repent means *to turn around*, and this challenge to turn around applies to the victim as much as to the abuser. The victim must also turn around, turn away from submission to the abuse. This act of turning is for the sake of the abuser as well as for the victim. Your father never set limits on your mother's way of constant invasion (which we call trespassing in the Lord's Prayer), and her personality and soul have become sicker through the years because of his acquiescence. What caused her to act this way originally I don't know. Perhaps she had deep childhood wounds that made her feel vulnerable, and she needed both to cling to and to exert power over those around her to give herself a sense of safety. But whatever the cause, you are injuring her further by not setting limits. Whether you 'speak the truth in love' alone with her or with your siblings, your pastor, or a family counselor present (I don't know which is best), it must be done."

The hard choices we need to make in the name of merciful righteousness must include such questions as these: Does forgiveness mean restoration and reconciliation? Just how do we set valid limits to what we will and will not permit? How do we "speak the truth in love"? Should we insist on restitution, compensation?

Forgiveness and reconciliation. Depth forgiveness may or may not lead to reconciliation and the restoration of a former relationship. As pointed out in chapter one, I have been struck by Jesus' curious toughness about forgiveness. He uses that word *forgiveness* only in situations in which the offender has not only felt remorse but has *repented*, which means to turn around and go in another direction. In cases where there has been no such repentance, Jesus speaks of loving and praying for the enemy, but he does not use the specific word *forgiveness*. When on the cross, as he looks at his *un*remorseful, *un*repentant executioners, he asks *God* to forgive them.

There are two kinds of forgiveness: one in which reconciliation and restoration are possible because repentance has been evidenced and the other in which we release the offender from our resentment but cannot restore the relationship because there has been no real change. Pamela Cooper-White elucidates the meaning of *reconciliation*:

> Reconciliation is often misunderstood in the church to mean an atmosphere of niceness and the suppression of conflict. . . . But this is contrary to the biblical sense of reconciliation. The three Greek words in the New Testament most often translated into English as "reconciliation" or "to reconcile" . . . mean a *thorough change*. To be reconciled is to be changed through and through.[1]

Saying "I am sorry" is not enough to bring about true reconciliation. The prerequisite to reconciliation is a turning around and a deep change.

In the prodigal son parable (Luke 15:11-32) no restoration was possible until the wasteful younger brother "came to himself," turned around, left the places he had been living as well as the way he had been living, and set his face toward home. His father, who obviously had been loving, waiting, watching for him, and upon seeing him from a distance ran to him in his eagerness, nevertheless had respected his son's free will. He had released him to make his own choices. If the young man had not turned around of his own free will, there could have been no reconciliation or restoration, no matter how deep the love of his father.

I knew a young assistant pastor who had been employed by a large church with a desperately overworked senior pastor. The older man constantly unloaded his fatigue and anger on his young assistant with sharp criticism, often in front of others, and made demeaning remarks behind the young man's back. The young pastor begged his employer to talk it over, to go with him to professional counseling, to pray together. The older pastor listened impatiently, insisting it was all in the young man's imagination or that he was too sensitive or that the criticisms were for his own good. Nothing changed. Eventually the younger pastor left his job.

"I think I've worked through my anger," he told me. "But it took a long time to build up any self-esteem again. I felt like such a failure. Also, I felt so sorry for *him*. He was way overworked, but he didn't know how to set any limits or prioritize. He looked desperately exhausted most of the time and tried so hard not to let his parishioners see it. But he was destroying me too. I didn't enter the ministry to be destroyed."

I remembered how Jesus left the towns that rejected and reviled him. He refused to curse them as his disciples urged, but he did shake the dust off his feet. Sometimes if we cannot physically shake off the dust, we may need to do so emotionally. I know a number of cases of unrepented childhood abuse in which the now-adult son or daughter has decided to remain in a relationship of courtesy and care, even compassion, but knows there can be no fullness of trust and intimacy. The true family, the dependable intimate friends, in such cases are outside the blood relationship.

I wonder if this is the emotional distancing that Jesus experienced, at least for a while, when his family tried to block his ministry, even have him restrained when they thought he had gone out of his mind (see Mark 3:21). He loved his family, but his trust and intimacy had to be placed elsewhere until there was a change on the part of family members: "Looking at those who sat around him, he said,

'Here are my mother and brothers! Whoever does the will of God is my brother and sister and mother'" (Mark 3:34-35).

If we have been the abuser and lost the trust of a friend or family member, though we grieve over that loss and admit its justice, we need to know that nevertheless we are a beloved child of God. A father I know had not protected his child against her abusive mother. He repented and asked forgiveness, but the daughter does not feel healed enough to bond with her father again and maintains a relationship of only cool politeness. He mourns the loss but knows his daughter may need many years of healing. He knows that God has forgiven him, and he prays that someday he and his daughter may be able to move on to a relationship that is not a restoration of the old but a new creation.

Setting valid limits. In this wounded and wounding world we will always be in some less-than-perfect relationships. Among the tough choices we make within healthy forgiveness is choosing to honor ourselves enough to expect courtesy and faith keeping from those with whom we live and work. If these expectations are violated, it is part of forgiveness to make clear, gently but firmly, what we will and will not tolerate. This stance is especially essential if we are returning to a relationship in which former hurts are healing.

In her book *The Verbally Abusive Relationship*, therapist Pat Evans points out that verbal abuse is not the same as ordinary conflict. Conflict is a disagreement regarding interests or the result of poor communication skills, which often can be resolved by those who together seek reasonable solutions. But abuse (of any kind) is a violation and a deliberate demeaning of another, which *cannot* be healed by reasonable discussion or even by the usual forms of counseling. This root difference explains why marriage, family, or job counseling so often fails. Abusiveness is an addiction to power exerted over another, and mere communication skills do not heal it. Setting limits is absolutely necessary in such cases.

When you set limits you speak from your own Personal Power, and you speak for the spirit of life at your center. You decide what is harmful and what is nourishing to your spirit. . . . For example, "I will not accept comments or 'jokes' which diminish or disparage me or put me down." It isn't easy for the partner of a verbal abuser to set limits because she must give up all her usual ways of seeking resolution and reconciliation—ways which . . . include explaining, trying to understand, trying harder to be understood, trying to figure out what went wrong.[2]

Evans points out that a simple, firm "stop it" is effective when the demeaning remarks begin. This approach does not mean that the people involved cannot discuss problems; it means that such discussion must be held with mutual respect.

Setting our valid limits definitely includes our firm, unapologetic claiming of the space and time we need for self-care and self-renewal. We have the need as well as the right to be in silence at times, to be alone at times, to think things over in our own way at our own pace, to enter into our "sabbaths" of relaxation and enjoyment. Self-care is not at all the same as selfishness. A selfish person who needs to grab and put "me first" on all occasions is usually a person who does *not* understand healthy self-care and the dignity of one's true needs.

Forgiveness

If we want forgiveness for our own past trespasses upon others, we need to ask God to help us understand why we have violated the freedom, dignity, and spaces of others. Were our own boundaries violated as a child? Do we demean others because we feel vulnerable and threatened if we don't? What are our bodily and emotional signals when we feel the urge to dominate and invade others? If we have a deep, chronic problem in our relationships, we probably will need professional therapeutic help to answer these questions. We will also need deep, healing prayer and the prayer of others, for this is a deep wound in ourselves which inflicts dangerous wounds on others.

"Speaking the truth in love" (Ephesians 4:15). I have read that for a former victim of an abusive situation to tell even one small lie to keep the peace is as dangerous as an alcoholic's taking one small drink.

We cannot afford any inner or outer deceptions about what is really happening, how we really feel, what we will and will not accept. Abuses of any kind depend on cover-ups. Any form of communal or individual forgiveness that consents to cover-ups is not forgiveness at all; it is corruption!

The truth must be named, as described in chapter two, where Jesus was quoted: "Nothing is covered up that will not be uncovered, and nothing secret that will not become known" (Luke 12:2).

Telling the truth does not mean vituperative yells. Emotional explosions usually make matters less clear, not more. Nor does telling the truth mean that we ignore the needs and feelings of others, even of our former abusers. We listen, trying to hear their heart, but we do not permit verbal or emotional violation. We keep right on speaking clearly about what we see happening and how we choose to act.

Suppose, for example, we choose to attend a reunion of our dysfunctional family, in which hurts are whispered about behind closed doors, and whatever is spoken aloud is usually a way of saying "you fool." (See Jesus' remarks about verbal abuse in Matthew 5:21-22.) How do we speak the truth in love in such an atmosphere?

First, we can ask the risen Christ to go ahead of us and prepare that potentially painful place for us and to stand with us as we enter that hurting and hurtful group. We might even ask him to stand between us and another person who may be draining us of energy or projecting hurtfulness on us.

When a family member whispers to us the latest mean thing someone else has said or done, we can reflect back to that person just what we are hearing. "This is what I am hearing you say, Aunt. How do you feel about it? What do you intend to do about it?" This neither makes excuses for the one responsible for the injury nor affirms the victimhood of the person confiding in us.

If another family member begins to make demeaning jokes, we can say, "I wonder what you are really feeling as you tell this hurtful joke? This is the way it makes me feel. . . ."

If another member of the family starts complaining and criticizing who we are or what we are doing, we can respond: "I'm sorry for both of us that you don't approve, but this is the way I see it, and this is my choice. If we can't talk it over with respect for each other, we'd better talk about something else."

Learning to respond with goodwill and clear firmness within a hurtful relationship can be as scary to a former victim as walking up to a hungry lion! To tell the truth in situations where we used to apologize, explain, prevaricate, blow up, flee in tears? Surely there will be disaster! There will only be fragmented pieces of us left!

Usually, in fact, we will be amazed at the power of good-humored truth telling. It will often be for us as it was for the prophet Daniel so many centuries ago, standing in the den of lions: "My God sent his angel and shut the lions' mouths so that they would not hurt me" (Daniel 6:22). Others are so often totally taken by surprise at hearing the truth spoken calmly and clearly that they will back off speechless or even be shocked into an honest, reflective response. If abusive reactions do continue, we can exercise our firm limit setting by merely smiling and walking away, saying, "I don't choose to stay with this." Jesus could tell us much about shaking the dust off our feet! (See Mark 6:11.)

When it comes to forgiveness given and received between wounding communities, churches, nations, political parties, ethnic groups, systems and organizations of all kinds, *the truth must be spoken.* It is definitely not enough to name the crimes of the past. They must be remembered and the naming must be continued at intervals. "Eternal vigilance is the price of liberty" is an old saying of profound wisdom. All communal powers without exception (including all religious communal bodies) are tempted constantly to violate, to trespass. The tragic irony is that the more sincere and idealistic the violators, the more they are tempted to trespass, to use force over others, to seek dominance over the inner spirit and not just the outer action, all for the "higher good" of those they are violating.

Trying to forgive a hurtful community or nation is useless unless the truth of its history is remembered, its truth told, and unless there are definite signs of its repentance, its turning around.

Should all things be forgiven? Are some acts unforgivable? How can one even think of forgiving ethnic holocausts? Isn't it obscene even to think of forgiving abuse of helpless children? How can anyone forgive the deliberate ruin of another person's life? These agonizing questions cannot be treated either sentimentally or superficially in the name of forgiveness.

Acts of cruelty and evil cannot be condoned or forgiven. The history of an act cannot be changed. It has done its work. Nor can the evil, dehumanizing ideologies that gave rise to those acts be forgiven. Rigid and loveless theologies, commercial greed, fanatical political and ethnic mind-sets that have led to inquisitions, witch-hunts, slave trading, and holocausts are unforgivable. God and the human wills set free by God eventually will dissolve these ideologies. Communal powers, nations, churches, industrial and political organizations that allow themselves to be corrupted by these dehumanizing ideologies and do not repent—turn around—also will be dissolved.

In the vision of time's end (Matthew 25:31-46), Jesus speaks of the nations gathered before God for discernment and judgment (verse 32), a judgment of communal powers, not individuals. Communal powers that have neglected and abused the vulnerable, the helpless, the hungry, and have not *re*formed will not survive. How many civilizations of the world already have been lost and forgotten?

God does not dissolve the individual. We stay in our self-made hell as long as we choose, as long as we ignore God's hand stretched out to help us. One of the books written by the Christian author C. S. Lewis, *The Great Divorce,* describes in fictional form how the souls in hell may take a bus to heaven whenever they choose. The spirits of the blessed meet them and plead with them to stay in heaven, but most of those from hell choose to return to their self-made hell because they are more comfortable in their glumness, self-pity, resentments, and because they are frightened at the bigness and solid *realness* of heaven and the painful growth required to become real and full of light.

As far as God is concerned, God still speaks to each of us as "my child," even as God spoke to the rich man in the parable of Lazarus.

Jesus does speak of a sin that cannot be forgiven:

Truly I tell you, people will be forgiven for their sins and whatever blasphemies they utter; but whoever blasphemes against the Holy Spirit can never have forgiveness, but is guilty of an eternal sin. (Mark 3:28-29)

If we understand the Holy Spirit, the Paraclete, as "the one who stands beside us, and calls us forth," this saying becomes more clear. If we refuse to turn to that one who stands by us, refuse that love and outstretched hand, if we refuse to come forth from our inner prisons—then there is no way we can be helped. We have refused the offered forgiveness, and thus it cannot heal our lives.

When we are the victims of radical evil, we are not asked to forgive the evil *act*. We are asked to remember that the perpetrator, even though trapped for now in the evil, is nonetheless a child of God. Even when we cannot yet forgive and release that other child of God, and perhaps cannot do so for a long time, we can deliver that person into God's hands, saying, "Loving God, at this time my hurt is so deep and my heart is so devastated with pain that I cannot even begin to forgive this person. It is enough for now to know that my wounder is in your hands, even as I am, and with you there is perfect understanding and recompense for all my pain. When the time is right, help me to begin my journey of healing and release." Such a prayer (in your own words, of course) is already well within the great unfolding of forgiveness.

When we are sickened by a news report of devastating hurt and evil done to another, we should not force ourselves to forgive on behalf of the victims. We can imagine, but we do not really know their own unique pain, and we do not know the unique strength from God pouring out to them. Nor do we know what goes on in the heart of the perpetrator. Our personal forgiveness is neither required nor even appropriate on behalf of another. Rather, we can pray the prayer of Jesus: "Father, forgive them; for they do not know what they are doing" (Luke 23:34). Or we can pray that God will somehow flood the awareness of the abuser with full consciousness of what has happened, so that repentance and transformation may happen. And certainly we should pray for the protection, healing, and guidance of the victim.

Is restitution possible? Even if an abuser or violator has shown remorse, proved repentance by changing his or her direction, has assumed financial responsibility for what has happened, told the truth to all involved, and given time, thought, and energy to repairing the damages, can the damage ever be undone?

In a sense we cannot ever make up for what we have done. Something real has been lost. Harm has happened. For example, if a person has experienced years of childhood neglect and rejection, a normal, happy childhood for that person is lost forever. The parents, even if fully aware and repentant, cannot restore that lost childhood even if a later relationship has become healed and close. Betrayal, infidelity to a spouse or friend, cannot be undone.

I neglected a dear friend once in the daily busyness of my life. She sent me a message saying she would like to see me. I thoroughly intended to go, but all sorts of other things came up I needed to attend to. I kept putting it off. Then she died, without having seen me. I realized then what I had left undone. My excuses were good ones, and knowing her, I knew she forgave me. Still, nothing could ever change the fact that I was not there by her bedside when she needed me. My choice became part of the universe, a fact that stood. "Forgive us our debts. . . ." This was a debt I could not ever repay.

I once read a poignant poem based on Jesus' story of the vineyard workers who came into the vineyard to work at the eleventh hour. They were welcomed by the employer and received the same pay as did those other workers who had come in at dawn and "borne the burden of the day and the scorching heat" (Matthew 20:12). The point of the story is the eager generosity of God who welcomes us abundantly no matter how tardy we may have been in our response. But, the poet muses sadly, whatever can make up for the loss of the joy "of those *morning* hours with Thee!"?

The prodigal son is welcomed back into his father's arms and home. He is given new clothes, a feast, and the house rings with the joy of his return. But he has squandered his inheritance, which he won't get twice, and now he will have to learn how to get along with his older brother, who is less than glad to see him again.

Forgiveness cannot change the past. But lest we feel that God has no answer other than to love us yet leave us with a sense of eternal loss, consider this bold vision: "So if anyone is in Christ, there is a new creation: everything old has passed away; see, everything has become new!" (2 Corinthians 5:17).

We are told that though our choices stand as unchangeable facts in the *old* universe, God offers us a *new* universe. We are still responsible for trying to make what restitution we can, for trying to heal wounds we have inflicted, but the crushing burden of guilt is lifted from us. The prison door is open, and that place we used to live is no longer our home. We are no longer the persons we were then. Who knows but that God will give us the joy of some *new* morning in a new vineyard to work within God's love!

The best reparation we can offer is to become compassionate toward those who mistreat us the way we mistreated others, releasing them from resentment. For example, the only true reparation I could make to my old friend whom I had neglected was to become more understanding of anybody who neglected me. Instead of taking offense at a friend who had forgotten or who was too busy to call or write me, I would try to remember how often I too had become distracted and overwhelmed by daily chores and neglected others. Then I would try to release that friend from the prison of my offendedness. I believe my old friend's beautiful spirit touched mine with this guidance. I remember the relief I felt when I realized I could do something real and valuable "in remembrance" of her.

This does *not* mean, however, that we should submit to abuse and victimization as reparation. Some years ago I knew of a son who had wounded his mother deeply with neglect and verbal abuse. He finally realized what was happening, repented, got professional help, and tried to become a loving, loyal son to her. In his remorse he went too far, turning himself into a slave to her every whim. Their relationship quickly became a toxic one, as she increasingly became the dictator and he the remorseful victim, forever trying to make up his earlier neglect of her. This is not righteous reparation; this is sickness. He did not understand or claim the dignity of a forgiven child of God but let his needs and valid boundaries be violated.

Sooner or later within our adventure of forgiveness, we will need to release our expectations that past history can be changed or compensated. It is an enormous step when we finally can say and believe: "That is past. Yes, something was lost, and harm was done. I grieve for it. But now, reborn within God's heart, I am in my true home. I am in a different spiritual and emotional universe. I see with different eyes and feast on new possibilities. I am a new person now, for God has called me 'out of darkness into his marvelous light'" (1 Peter 2:9).

This awareness, this good news, is the deep fulfillment of our hunger and thirst for righteousness.

~

Suggested Meditation for Discerning Choices within Forgiveness

Blessed are those who hunger and thirst
for righteousness,
for they will be filled (Matthew 5:6).

For this meditation of listening and discernment, you may wish to have paper and pencil with you to write down the inner guidance you feel. You may also plan to discuss any inner direction that comes to you with a trusted friend or group.

Sit or lie down in a posture that makes deep listening easy, with your spine straight and supported. Of course, you can take a walk if movement helps to clear your thoughts and prepares you for inner listening. Breathe slowly and very deeply without straining or pushing, two or three times, then let your breath come gently and naturally.

Give thanks for the presence of the risen Jesus Christ who was not afraid to make clear, hard choices within his life of love. Ask for his guidance.

When you feel ready, ask inwardly (or write down): What are the choices I need to make about this person or these persons? What are my God-guided options in this toxic situation? Is this a relationship or commitment that can be healed and restored?

Has there been any sign of real change, not mere remorse or just ignoring the problem. Are there any real signs of hope and new life? What is happening to my bodily health, my hopefulness, my vitality, in this relationship and situation? Is the light in me becoming darkness? Is God calling me out?

Take as much time as you need with these last questions. You may need to come back to the rest of the meditation at a later time.

If you are ready to proceed, ask yourself in God's presence and strength, If I feel I can stay with this situation, how can I give myself space for my healing? a temporary separation? an inner withdrawal for a while? a center in my home where I can go for daily renewal?

When ready, ask these questions: What valid limits and boundaries can I set in this situation? What is unacceptable to me in the words and acts of others? When these borders are trespassed upon, how may I respond from God's gentle power rather than with attack or defense?

When you feel ready to move on, think of some upcoming difficult encounter. Ask yourself: How can I speak the clear truth in this encounter in a spirit of love? What will that sound like? How will my body feel?

If you are the wounder learning to forgive yourself, move through all these suggested questions, and then ask, What is the best restitution I can make, whether to this person or to others in his or her name? Pray for God's help that your restitution flows from your center of dignity as a loved and forgiven child of God.

If you are the wounded, ask yourself if you are ready to release the one who hurt you from your expectations and the burden of your resentment. If this is not the right time, you can come back to this question later. Do not push yourself.

If you do feel ready to release the other, think of a prison door within you opening wide. Your offender walks out of the open door, leaves your body and spirit, and walks along his or her path in freedom. You are also free and released from that weight. Ask the living Christ to enter that former prison cell of resentment, to heal it with his blessing and fill it with his light. Let that place be transformed into a beautiful chapel where a votive light always shines, and the windows are open to let in the freshness of God's air. Or let that cell be transformed into a beautiful garden with free birds flying, flowers opening, healing springs flowing. You can visit your chapel or pray in your garden whenever you choose.

If inner envisioning is difficult for you, you can draw or paint a picture of inner release of the other, or you can use words of release, such as: "In the name of the living Christ, I set you free from my resentment and my expectations. Go on your way in peace. Thanks be to God who sets us free."

Take a few more moments of rest and take slow, refreshing breaths. How does your body feel? Do you notice any change? If you sense that any bodily part has especially internalized and borne the burden of resentment (such as your back muscles, your abdomen, your heart, your shoulders, your eyes), gently touch those parts (if you can) or ask the healing Christ, the Liberator, to touch them. Our bodies too have been held in the prison of smoldering resentment. Tell your body it is being set free from this dark inner prison, this heavy weight.

You may wish to repeat to yourself this wonderful stanza from the hymn "And Can It Be that I Should Gain":

Forgiveness

Thine eye diffused a quickening ray;
I woke, the dungeon flamed with light;
my chains fell off, my heart was free,
I rose, went forth, and followed thee.

—Charles Wesley

Give thanks to God, yawn, lightly massage face and hands. Come gently into reentry.

CHAPTER SIX

Seeing the Wounds of Our Wounders

Blessed are the merciful,
for they will receive mercy.
— Matthew 5:7

*A*t some point within our journey of forgiveness will come the first impulse of mercy. For some it comes within minutes; for others that impulse may come years later.

Too often we have been taught that forgiveness begins *only* when we first feel mercy. The major point of this book is that this whole journey of healing and release *is* the path of forgiveness. Somewhere along that path mercy begins to unfold.

In the ancient city of Jerusalem, mercy was at the very center of the city and nation in an astounding, symbolic way. In the heart of the great Temple there was a small curtained room, considered the site of awesome power, known as the holy of holies. The Hebrews believed God's actual presence abided in that sacred space.

Within the curtained room stood the ark of the covenant, a rectangular box containing the scrolls of God's divine law. On top of the ark lay a slab of gold, called the mercy seat. At each end of the mercy seat knelt two carved angels, cherubim (the angels closest to God), facing each other with wings outspread.

"There I will meet with you . . . ," God promised his people (Exodus 25:22).

Once a year the high priest of the Temple entered the holy of holies and there behind the curtain prayed to God on behalf of the people and sprinkled the blood of a perfect animal seven times as the sign of God's forgiveness of sin and mercy toward the whole nation. The Hebrews believed this mercy and forgiveness radiated with power from the heart of the Temple outward into the hearts and lives of all the people of God.

Directly in front of the curtained area stood an altar with curved horns at each corner. Anyone fleeing from captivity could grasp the horns of the altar with both hands and cling there, claiming mercy.

Near this altar stood a tall lampstand shaped as the tree of life, and on the altar lay loaves of fresh bread, renewed daily, known as the bread of the presence, symbolizing God's unfailing nourishment of the people.

Was Jesus thinking of these loaves fresh each day, this bread of the presence, when he told us to pray, "Give us this day our daily bread"? Surely he was thinking not only of our bodily need for bread (though that too was extremely important in his life and teaching) but also what it stood for—God's gift of renewed spiritual life each day.

Both Jesus and those who heard him knew of that radiating center of mercy and renewal symbolized by the Temple of Jerusalem.

"You are that temple," wrote Saint Paul years later to the early Christian churches. The early Christians never meant to abolish a central holy of holies, a mercy seat, but to fling open the door and give holiness to all people everywhere. "Do you not know that you are God's temple and that God's Spirit dwells in you? . . . God's temple is holy, and *you are that temple*" (1 Corinthians 3:16-17, italics mine).

It is almost impossible for us to grasp the explosive impact those words had in the early church. We don't have an equivalent experience. The shock would have been a bit like our reaction today if someone said—and meant it literally, "You are a walking solar energy plant!" or "You have the power of the neutron bomb!"

But the revelation meant much more, because people believed that the Temple held not only God's awesome creative power but also God's even more awesome *mercy*!

And we *are* that temple! Within us radiates God's holy of holies. God's holy law is implanted deep within our heart. Within us, body and soul, grows the tree of life. Within us the bread of the presence is daily renewed. Above all, within each of us shines the pure gold of the mercy seat, where the cherubim (higher than the archangels) kneel.

"There I will meet with you," God says to us.

In the early stages of forgiveness, most of us do not yet see or feel the full power of the mercy within us. In the beginning of our journey, it is enough to know that though we ourselves do not yet feel the mercy, nevertheless the risen Christ is already within us as our mercy seat. And even as the high priest sprinkled blood seven times in that holy place, so do we bring our heart's blood of pain to that place of mercy and discover that God's own heart's blood already is poured out for us in that holy place where law and mercy meet. Andrew Sung Park reminds us:

> God suffers not because sin is all powerful, but because God's love for humanity is too ardent to be apathetic toward suffering humanity. No power in the universe can make God vulnerable, but a victim's suffering breaks the heart of God. . . . God's love for humans suffers on the cross. The cross represents God's full participation in the suffering of victims. . . . The cry of the wounded heart of God on the cross reverberates throughout the whole of history.[1]

In Revelation, the last book of the Bible, John tells how an angel showed him God's high throne (a symbol of God's ultimate power) and from that throne flowed a crystal-bright, healing river of life (Revelation 22:1-2). That ever-flowing river nourishes the tree of life whose leaves will bring about "the healing of the nations."

As I read this powerful vision, it sounds as if the pure gold of the mercy seat not only radiates but flows forth like a river into our lives. It does even more! A Jewish scholar once told me that the merciful power of the holy of holies not only shone out from the Temple, but like a great central magnet, drew *toward* it all the impurities and sins of the nation to be cleansed, healed, and transformed.

Seeing the Wounds of Our Wounders

As I reflect on the powerful meanings of the mercy seat, I think of another shrine of healing opened to the world more than a century ago. Young Bernadette of Lourdes, France, under divine guidance from a vision of Mary, scratched a hole in the mud floor of a grotto near the area where each day the blood-soaked bandages from the hospital were dumped and burned. When the vision of Mary told her to drink from the spring of water in that corner, at first she found nothing but damp mud as she dug with her fingers. That night a man blind in one eye went secretly to the grotto and pressed some of the wet mud against his eye—and went screaming back to town that he could see! The next day the villagers saw a thin trickle of water bubbling up from that spot. Someone got a shovel and dug until a stream of water the size of a child's arm gushed forth. Soon the stream was yielding a hundred liters of water a minute, then it expanded to a hundred thousand liters a day. This spring at Lourdes continues to flow unceasingly for the healing of hundreds in both body and spirit.

In the way that the ancient Temple both drew pain and sin toward the holy center and radiated outward God's healing power, so do the waters of Lourdes, having sprung up in the place of infected wounds, draw thousands of the sick to its center and yet flow forth without ceasing.

It is exactly the same with our own inner healing. God's heart of endless mercy shines like light within and around us, draws our pain and darkness to the healing source, and flows like a river of life into our body, our daily life, and to those around us. Some of us experience this mercy at first only as a slight trickle, a thin thread of change. Others of us already feel a vast abundant river of mercy.

Slowly, spontaneously, we begin to see with God's eyes and feel with God's heart. Recently a woman talked to me about beginning to feel the healing of her self-esteem and confidence. She still carries the scars of her prolonged emotional wounding from her husband during twenty-four years of a destructive marriage. "All along," she told me, "even in the midst of the hurt and anger, I kept feeling a sorrow for him, which I didn't quite understand. I've recently been thinking about what he went through as a baby and a little boy. His mother left him when he was only two. Even before she left she had turned his care over to servants or boarded him out to child-care homes for weeks at a time.

"His father meant well but didn't know how to comfort him or get close to him emotionally. When he was about five, his father married again, a beautiful, brilliant professional woman, an expert in children's early education. She not only punished little John harshly, both bodily and emotionally, she also sexually abused him when he grew a bit older. Either his father really didn't know what was going on, or he felt powerless to stop her. His own mother wrote him only once in all those years and never attempted to see him.

"He was never healed of all this. Though he was brilliant intellectually, his self-confidence was nonexistent. He did go to some therapists after I married him, and he was bright enough, educated enough, to discuss his problems intellectually. But he never trusted them (or me) enough to open his deep heart of pain and fear. Perhaps he simply didn't dare. The only way he could survive as a little child was to keep his heart defended and trust no one! The only place where he felt safe to dump his darkness was on *me*, in bursts of irrational fury. I can see now that there is still a scared, bewildered little boy trapped inside his grown-up man's body."

We see such projections of early hurt and anger in many relationships: parents to children, friend to friend, teacher to student, student to teacher, pastor to parishioner, parishioner to pastor, among professional colleagues, in daily business interchanges, in the stores, on the highways between drivers.

Sometimes the projected fear and anger are deeply destructive and sometimes, trivial. Such fear and anger can extend over years or erupt within seconds. These feelings are not always expressed through bursts of inappropriate anger; they can also manifest through trivializing, teasing, barbed joking, scorn and contemptuous demeaning, ignoring, silent treatment, sarcastic little comments, and so forth. The underlying cause is usually the urge to control and demean another person as a means of defense against the scary confrontation of inner fear and anger. Such behavior is not usually a freely chosen action; it is a *re*action to something that triggers the deep frightening feelings within. Often the offender will not even remember later just what happened, what he or she said or did during this instinctive reaction.

Once we begin to understand the source of the abuse we have experienced, we do not condone or allow the abuse. We do begin to feel sorrow and compassion for the terrified child within the abuser.

Sometimes we see that child within the other even in the midst of the abusive experience. A minister told me what he suddenly sensed while a parishioner was sharply criticizing him in front of other parishioners. "At that very moment while she was trying to dominate and control me, trying to put me down in the meanest way, I could see a panicky little girl, staring terrified through those sixty-year-old eyes, a little girl who was trying so hard to make everything and everybody around her perfect, so that she would feel safe, so that she would be loved. All of a sudden I didn't dislike her so much anymore. I found myself even trying in my heart to reach out to that frightened child and pray for her!"

Slowly it begins. We think of a driver who has just made a rude sign as he zooms by to cut us off on the highway. The anger spurts up, yes, but so do questions (whether within two minutes or two hours): What went on in his home today? What went on in his home as a child—day after day? We look into a murderer's face on television news and after our first normal reaction of shock and horror over what he or she did, our next thought might be: What happened to you somewhere along the line? What built up such rage from your babyhood on?

"Love your enemies and pray for those who persecute you" (Matthew 5:44)? As stressed earlier, this challenge does not mean that we become powerless victims to our wounders, even when we do begin to feel the river of compassion. It does mean that we begin to see and think about our offenders through God's eyes as well as our own. We begin to see their deep pain or their numb or insensitive armor against pain, the way God has seen it all along.

We begin to see others through God's eyes—our hurtful family groups, our battling religious groups, ethnic groups, nations. We begin to ask: What wounded this communal body so deeply that centuries of persecutions, outrages, revenge, rose from its pain? Or what destructive ideology possessed this communal body, like a demonic spirit, making it sick and twisted?

Even when we may need wars or legal procedures to save lives, God still asks us to hold in our deep hearts the vision of a communal soul acting out its rage, fear, and hurt just as an unhealed individual does. Even when we need forcibly to restrain a dangerous person or group, we can learn to say inwardly: God sees your inner pain; God hears your inner crying; God knows your inner terror. May God help me to see it, hear it, know it also.

In her powerful, poignant book *Taking Back My Yesterdays,* Linda Hollies describes tearfully a sudden, surprising reflection while thinking of her father who had abused her. Her tears reflected sorrow not only for her father as an individual but sorrow over the pain of a family and a larger ethnic suffering. As she wept in mercy she received what she gave—a heart softened and expanded within her.

> One day the tears came. . . . I cried for the loss of his childhood. His mother died and his father "got lost" before he was seven years old. . . . I cried for him having to fend for himself. . . . In this huge extended and dysfunctional family, my father tried to find a place to be somebody. No parents, no siblings, no one to watch his back. I cried for him. He needed my tears. I cried for the dark color of his skin and the searching brilliance of his sharp mind. . . . Black was not beautiful. To the world his dark skin equaled inferiority and lack of ability. . . . I cried for the lack of affirmative action and equal opportunity which imprisoned him in a laborer's

job at the steel mills for thirty-five years. He had hopes and dreams. . . . He wanted to contribute and be recognized. But the nation was too closed. . . . I cried for him. He needed my tears. . . . Did the tears absolve his sins toward me? Of course not! . . . Did the tears heal my wounded spirit and mend my broken heart? Not quite. But it was the beginning of my *taking back my yesterdays!* The tears began to melt the hate which had gathered for too long around my heart. The tears begin to wash my mind of the aged unforgiveness. The tears helped me to view the other side of my father's story. He was dead and had been dead for over twelve years. But he needed my tears. And I cried for him.[2]

Sometimes we do not discover any evidence of real wounding in the background of our victimizer. No trauma or broken heart seems to explain the abusive behavior. What then? Is compassion appropriate? In the first place, of course, we simply do not know what wounds and scars another person may be carrying, even though he or she outwardly appears free of deep hurt. In the second place, other formative powers besides wounds can infect one's life.

Moral sleep is one such influence. Many people simply have not woken up, become empathetic toward others. For example, the Roman soldiers who drove the nails into Jesus' hands and feet, and who probably had done the same thing to other people, felt they were just doing their job. The agony and cries of victims simply did not reach them. They were unconscious of the fact that they held in their hands a human being as alive, as real as they were. The pain of the other was not a relevant reality. In truth, they knew not what they did.

As a little child I once pulled off the wings of a fly. I was not angry at the fly. I simply was curious what a flying thing would do if it had no wings! It didn't dawn on my four-year-old consciousness that this little creature was suffering pain. It was merely an object for me to experiment with. When I grew older, I was horrified as I looked back on what I did because a moral empathy had awakened within me. For some it seems *not* to awaken. If we sense this lack of empathy in someone who has injured us, the river of compassion beginning to flow within us will guide us to pray: God of love, I sense this person really does not understand what she [or he] is doing. Help me to feel mercy toward her [or his] closed-off, sleeping heart. In your mercy, help this person to wake up and come into awareness of what she [or he] does.

Another great source of abusiveness is becoming infected, invaded, possessed by an ideology, a group mentality, a mob spirit, a religious or political fanaticism that envelops the human spirit and overrides any individual resistance. This kind of possession can invade a small group, a family, a church, even a whole nation. The individual members become convinced that what they are doing is God's will or for the good of the political party or for the well-being of the state or for the purity of the ethnic group or for the salvation of everyone's soul. They simply are not thinking or feeling as individuals anymore. Was Judas one of these people possessed by group ideology? Had he become so possessed by the mind-set of the revolutionary group known as the Zealots that everything, including Jesus, became a means to his party's ends?

If we have evidence that the one who injures us is acting out of a fanatical ideology, we need to pray with both compassion and power that this person may be *released* from the grip of the obsessing and possessing mental and spiritual power controlling him or her. We need to pray also for ourselves that we be kept free from the fanatical fears and hatreds that up to present times seek to infect and control us through the mail, cult-dominated printing presses, and increasingly through the internet.

A feeling of powerlessness and intimidation can be another major source of abusiveness. In recent years there was a horrifying case of a small child abused, tortured, and eventually killed by a stepfather. The mother of the child, basically a good person, was so terrified and disempowered over the years by her husband that she was almost totally benumbed. She saw what was happening to her little girl but believed there was nothing in the world she could do about it. Quite properly she was legally accused of consenting to the crime, but the evil in her case was rooted in terror and a sense of powerlessness. This sense of powerlessness is more widespread than we realize. Many abuses in families and abuses in schools, churches, job places, and nations arise because the basically good people involved feel they are powerless to stop the evil. Sometimes this powerlessness is expressed in tears, sometimes in weak attempts to comfort the victims and to propitiate the abuser, and sometimes by totally closing one's eyes in denial.

When we sense that we are being injured because of someone's weakness and helplessness in the face of evil, again—

from the power of God's mercy seat—we can pray that this person, these people, may be released from their own stance as victim and be empowered by God's spirit not only to weep but to act.

Does no one act from a free choice of will? Doesn't abuse sometimes arise not from wounds, not from lack of moral awareness, not from party spirit, not from powerlessness, but from deliberate expediency, plain desire for power, from straightforward selfishness and self-aggrandizement? I do not deny the possibility, even the probability. I have met a few people who seem to do evil, knowing what they do, but of course I do not know what may have happened in their lives. But if this free choice of evil is true for some, they are to be the most pitied of all.

If people truly know what they do and choose evil anyway, they are caught in a prison of self-destruction that almost defies description. They are defiling their own inner holy of holies. They are smashing the mercy seat (even as the physical holy of holies and mercy seat were defiled and smashed by the Roman armies who eventually destroyed Jerusalem a generation after Jesus' death). They are trying to cut off the great river of healing that flows from God's heart. How does one pray with compassion for the deliberate, unwounded offender who *knows* what he or she does?

As I struggle with this question, the only thing that comes to me is the memory of a strange dream I had some years ago. I was sitting on the floor in a room where Jesus was talking to us. Jesus in the dream was a medium-tall, black man. Someone came through the door, a tall woman with a face as white as ice. She brought with her almost palpable waves of cold, deliberate cruelty. Jesus rose to his feet when she entered. She looked at him, laughed, and said something in a soft, mocking voice concerning his crucifixion, which I could not hear. He stood looking her silently in the face, and I could feel an enormous intensity rising in the room around them. I left quietly, knowing this was no place for me. I whispered to myself in awe outside the room, "She actually thinks she can *mess with* Jesus!" (Not my usual language, but those were my words.)

What happened then in that room? I don't know. The dream did not tell me. I did know that whatever had passed between Jesus and the woman, Jesus had within him the full power of God's own heart not to destroy but to encounter the evil heart with his own white-hot heart of transforming love.

I do not know how Jesus transforms evil, but he has promised it will be done and is even now being done. So the best I can do when up against what appears to be deliberate, freely chosen evil is to envision the victimizer alone in the room with Jesus—and leave them there together. Perhaps this is the ultimate intercessory prayer from the mercy seat.

If we ourselves have been victimizers for whatever reason—our wounds, our ignorance, our denial and powerlessness, or our free and deliberate choice—it is even more vital that we claim the mercy seat within us. In our own heart we can grasp those carved horns on the altar as did the guilty in ancient times and let the radiant release flow to us from God's holy of holies. The earlier we grasp hold of God's mercy the better, even *before* we name our abusiveness, even before we repent and make restitution.

Then within that sanctuary we can look more fully at

what we have done. Within that safe place of God's presence, we can ask for help in understanding why we did what we did or did not do what was needed. What hurt us so deeply that we needed to hurt others? What ignorance made us think we had acted righteously? What possessing power over us made us feel helpless? Finding these answers is not the same as excusing ourselves. It is the wish to *understand* ourselves that allows us to stop the vicious cycle of hurt and learned powerlessness passed on to others through each day or down through the generations.

Clinging to God's mercy seat, we can visualize the hurtful person we were in some past event, speak to the person we were at that moment, hold forth the merciful power and love of God to that abusive person we were, and offer the healing release from whatever rage, fear, or woundedness drove us to our abusiveness. We can envision ourselves as we are now offering both the bread of the presence and the water of life to that unfree person we used to be, whether yesterday, last year, or fifty years ago.

If we cannot understand what drove us to wound others, if all we can see is our desire to violate and hurt, we can cling inwardly to that altar of mercy and ask the living Christ to come to us there in the holy of holies where the law and the mercy come together.

"There I will meet with you," God has promised.

Clinging to the Holy One whose name is love, a new creation will begin.

~

Suggested Meditation for Seeing the Wounds in Others

Blessed are the merciful,
for they will receive mercy (Matthew 5:7).

It may be a long time before you are ready for this meditation. In the preceding meditation you may have found yourself able and ready to release your wounder from your inner prison of resentment, setting yourself free as well. In this meditation, however, you will be facing your wounder again in a new way. You are now at the point where you can begin to see the wounder's own inner pain and to pray for the healing of those wounds. Take the time you need and do not push yourself. You can always return to this meditation later.

But if you feel ready, surround yourself with the full light of God's love (imagine, for example, wrapping yourself in Jesus' cloak) and speak to the Merciful One, asking that the way to mercy be prepared.

If envisioning helps you, go with the Healer to your inner chapel, your garden, or some other place that feels both safe and beautiful.

When ready, let Christ the Healer invite the one who hurt you into your safe place. Let that person come in the form of his or her inner wound or the part that has been morally asleep, felt powerless, or been possessed by an ideology. The inner problem may come as a frightened, crying, lost, angry, or bewildered little girl or boy. Or the inner hurt and problem may come as a wilted, neglected flower or shrub. Or it may come as an injured animal.

You may wish to draw, paint, sculpt, or write down what you feel to be the hurt or problem in the other person. Do *not* try to dance it or take it into your body in any way. Only the risen Jesus may safely take the wounds or unfreedom of other people into his own body.

Envision the Christ bringing the hurt of the other person into the circle of healing light. Envision the Christ anointing that hurt with healing oil, saying, "Child of God, be healed [awakened, set free, empowered]."

If a whole community has hurt you: a family, a church, an ethnic group, a workplace; or if a wound has come down through generations, try to picture the communal body as one hurt or trapped person. How does this being look? What facial expression do you see? Do not take this communal darkness into your body in any way. Instead, envision the Christ embracing this communal being, anointing it with healing oil, taking its pain into his own heart, wakening it, setting it free.

If inner envisioning is hard for you, you can put this prayer into words inwardly spoken, such as: Child of God, whatever inner hurt or unfreedom caused you to hurt me, I release you to the hands of the living Christ, the Healer. May you be anointed with healing oil, awakened and empowered. May your deepest needs be met. I pray this in the strong, transforming name of Jesus.

If it is for your own self you seek mercy, bring your wound to the hands and the heart of Christ. Bring the person you were who was hurtful to others to God's mercy seat where God has promised to meet us.

Ask Christ the Healer to mingle his blood with yours as in a divine transfusion. Sense the empowered new life circulating through your whole body, personality, spirit. Sense how it cleanses what needs cleansing, heals what needs healing, awakens that which is asleep, sets free that which has been trapped and obsessed, empowers that which has felt victimized.

If such envisionings do not help you, you can pray inwardly: Merciful Healer, enter those deep, dark places from which my hurtfulness has come. Touch my hidden wounds, awaken me, set me free, empower me with your new life, enfold me in your mercy. I pray you also heal and enfold those whom I have hurt. I pray in the strong power of your name.

Come gently forth from this meditation. Stretch and breathe slowly and deeply of God's breath. The Healer, the Comforter, still enfolds you and renews you.

Gently massage face, hands, and wrists, and reenter your daily life.

Chapter Seven

Focusing on God's Light in Others and Ourselves

*Blessed are the pure in heart,
for they will see God.*

—Matthew 5:8

I had a strange experience recently at an airport X-ray checkpoint. Returning from a retreat, I carried in my hand luggage three bronze medallions showing scenes from the life of Jesus. The X ray immediately picked up the strangely shaped metal. The young woman examiner politely asked me to come to the table where she could search my bag.

"Oh, yes, I forgot," I told her. "I have some religious medallions in here." I pulled out the tissue-wrapped articles and started to hand them to her. Instantly she drew back without touching them.

"Have they been blessed?" she asked me.

"Well, I don't really know," I answered, rather startled. "They feel blessed to *me*, but I don't know if there was an official ceremony."

She shook her head. "Then I won't touch them. You unwrap them and show them to me. If they have been blessed my touch would desecrate them."

"How could your touch possibly desecrate them?" I asked. "Here you are all day, every day, working in front of these X-ray machines to help keep us all safe. I think your touch could only add to their blessedness!"

But she firmly shook her head, looked at them closely while I held them, and permitted me to go on through the checkpoint.

Concern for purity, noncontamination, is a live issue even in our modern culture, though I had not seen it take this form before. One hears racial supremacists ranting about purity of bloodlines, even though we should have outgrown that evil nonsense centuries ago. We hear a lot about purity in advertisements for food, soaps, cosmetics. It is a hopeful sign that we begin to care about pollution in our water, air, and soil.

Essentially purity means singleness, oneness, a central focus. Among the orthodox in Jesus' time, the central focus on God was expressed by establishing many rules about what one ate, what one touched, involving all one's actions. The orthodox felt themselves called to be a pure, uncontaminated people in covenant with God. But Jesus, and many of the major prophets as well, felt that purity of life, the single focus on God, was not defined by rules about outer action. Purity went much deeper: "There is nothing outside a person that by going in can defile, but the things that come out are what defile. . . . For it is from within, from the human heart, that evil intentions come" (Mark 7:15, 21).

Therefore, Jesus was totally unconcerned about contamination when bleeding women touched him or when he laid hands on dead people or healed foreigners or sat down at table with "sinners." He certainly would not have considered the touch of an honest, hardworking airport examiner to be desecration.

Jesus looks at what goes on in the heart. He is concerned with our priorities, our motives and intentions. He warns us that if we split our energies, if we try to serve two conflicting purposes, if we say one thing and do another, we are living dangerously fractured lives.

Within our forgiveness journey, we need the singleness, the purity of heart that focuses on the radiant central light, the source of our strength. Without this constant focusing and refocusing throughout the day, I doubt if we can endure, let alone move with transforming power through the pain, anger, sorrow, shame, and guilt of depth forgiveness.

Many of us have had to learn this during bodily pain and struggle. It is even more essential in the emotional pain of forgiveness to center on God's light around us, within us, and shining (though perhaps only dimly) in each person we meet.

In the preceding chapter I described the mercy seat, both light and magnet, drawing all sins and wounds toward this healing center for cleansing and transformation. This is exactly what our bodily hearts are doing. From the heart the cleansed and nourishing blood is pumped outward through the arteries into every organ, every cell. Back through the veins the exhausted, impure blood flows toward the heart, is cleansed in the lungs, and is restored to the heart's chambers from which it is sent forth again, clean and renewed.

At various times throughout the day, I take a few moments to focus on my breathing and think of breathing not only air but God's spirit (*spirit* and *breath* are the same word in Hebrew), envisioning it flowing to all parts of my body. I also envision my hurts, my sins, or any toxicity I may have absorbed during the day flowing to the shining center that is God. I ask God to cleanse, heal, and renew these energies, and to send them forth again as transformed empowerment.

Sometimes I place my open palms over my heart while I envision this inner cycle of cleansing and healing. Such an inner recentering can be done frequently throughout the day, if only for a few minutes each time. I try to remember first to take a few slow, deep breaths without pushing or gasping, then let the breath become gentle and natural.

We can take a few moments of sabbath rest during the day in many ways. For example, at least once an hour we can relax our bodies, stretch slowly and gently, and yawn deeply. Yawning does three important things for us: it lets in a deep lungful of fresh oxygen; it lets out a lungful of carbon dioxide; and it relaxes the tight jaw muscle, which is the most powerful voluntary muscle of the body. We can gaze out the window for a few minutes, deliberately appreciating a tree, a cloud, a bird, the color of the sky. We can touch with gentleness and appreciation some part of our bodies (eyes, hands, feet, heart) that has been working hard for us. We can close our eyes and pay attention to our breathing and then say a line or two from a hymn or poem or a verse from scripture or just our own private prayer to God. We can smell a flower; eat a piece of fruit; sing a song; gently massage our face, hands, wrists, arms, giving thanks to God for the gifts of the bodily senses.

Another powerful and transforming way of remaining focused on God is to begin to see God's presence within the people around us: God's light around them and the wonderful potential within them. The preceding chapter suggested learning to envision the woundedness in our enemy or in any difficult or hurtful person, but we can go deeper. We can begin to see our enemy as God might—healed, made whole, reflecting God's loving light.

This thought came to me some years ago when I was working on a church program with a touchy, easily offended colleague. He interpreted everything I said as a personal affront. His inner hurt child was only too obvious. Suddenly I inwardly asked: What would this man be like if he were healed of suspicion and offendedness? What would the expression on his face be like if he were relaxed and trustful? What would he be like if he were revealing God to me?

It was a vision of splendor! I began to see deeper than this man's wounds. I saw a man confident in his self-worth as God's child, sharing freely the joy and laughter as well as the keen wit and intelligence that were his own special gifts.

There was no instant miraculous change in him, but I felt very differently about him. I noticed also a marked difference in the emotional atmosphere in the room, almost as if I had stepped into a more spacious place and was breathing a different air. Also as the day went on I did feel as if a door were opening gradually in his tight constriction, as if he too were sensing a larger, freer space.

This insight was a great gift to me, and I began to understand how Jesus looked into the deep heart and soul of Simon, that blundering, overcontrolling fisherman, and saw Peter there, the Peter whose passionate love and loyalty became the rock of the church.

Silently, asking to see with the eyes of God, we can inwardly speak to that hidden splendor within the other: You are a child of God, and your deep inner light from God is beautiful. May you and your unique gift be healed so that your original empowered beauty may shine forth.

What we envision in the other person might look very much like our concept of an angel of God!

We can pray this prayer for ourselves too, asking to envision or sense the presence of God's splendor within ourselves. What would we be like as healed persons? How would we feel? How might our expressions or voices change?

A woman once told me: "I'm a worrywart and a control freak! The other day my grown children were preparing for an outing with their families. I was rushing around, fussing, advising, warning, arranging, all nonstop. Then, all of a sudden, I had this inner picture of what it would be like if I were free of this anxiousness, this need to 'fix it.' I saw myself as a relaxed, smiling person, waving good-bye to them at the door, coming back peacefully into the house, trusting their good sense to take care of themselves and have a good time. I could feel myself actually moving into that picture, that atmosphere—at least a little. It wasn't that I was making myself do or be something. It was more like seeing what God sees when

God looks at me deep down. I think my young people felt a change in the atmosphere too!"

This way of inwardly seeing ourselves and others is not the same as willpower. It is not contrivance. It is not a way of forcing ourselves or another person into a desired mold. It is a new way of looking at ourselves. Perhaps we could call it looking at ourselves or another from God's perspective, seeing the inner light, seeing the potentiality. It is the vision of purity. "The eye is the lamp of the body. So, if your eye is healthy, your whole body will be full of light" (Matthew 6:22).

This way of seeing is not the same as denial. Denial is a self-made form of blindness to whatever feels threatening and uncomfortable. To see from the pure eye definitely is not a rejection of clear and unpleasant truths. The cleansed vision of forgiveness sees the ugly situation, calls it by name, makes hard choices, sees the wounds, but also sees the hidden splendor within each child of God, including ourselves.

There are many ways of seeing God, at least in ways our limited minds can grasp. Christians believe we see directly into the heart and nature of God when we focus on Jesus Christ.

> It is the God who said, "Let light shine out of darkness," who has shone in our hearts to give the light of the knowledge of the glory of God in the face of Jesus Christ." (2 Corinthians 4:6)

Some of us see that face in our imaginings, in our heart. Some of us see that face in the actual transforming changes we experience in our life. Some of us see that face shining from the faces, words, and loving acts of other people. Some of us dream of that face. Some of us feel vividly that presence in our prayers or at times when we are in deep need. Often, those who consider themselves the least worthy, the most impure, see the risen Jesus *directly,* which is the way he has always acted—astounding the sinner, scandalizing the righteous.

For example, a beloved friend of mine whom I have known for many years told me (and has given permission to share this story) that over forty years ago she stood in despair in her child's bedroom. Her baby was asleep in the crib; otherwise she was alone in the room, standing, gazing toward the window. "I felt just drowned," she told me. "I had made a mess of my own life. I had let everybody down. I had made every mistake in the book. I felt my life was ruined, and the despair was cold and horrible. Then I saw him. He was standing at the end of the room between me and the window, wearing a brown robe with a rope tied around his waist, and thong sandals on his feet. I couldn't see his actual features, but the love, and above all, the *warmth* that flowed from him was beyond anything I had ever imagined possible. Everything changed for me that moment.

"There were a lot of hard things I still had to go through, but I knew I was completely loved and I was totally forgiven. And the amazing thing was that I hadn't even been praying! I wasn't even thinking of him. But he came anyway, and I saw him."

Yes, this happens. It happens amazingly often. I have heard it over and over. It is one of the best-kept secrets of the church—the real presence of Jesus the Christ—not just as a memory, not just as a historical inspiration, not just as a metaphor, but the real person who continues to show us the face of God.

My friend had thought herself too impure to experience the love of God, but her inner eye of longing and receptivity was more open than she knew. Her heart was ready for healing. And she saw God.

Most of us may not see God in the way she did. That was God's response to her special need in the way that was best for her. Each of us will see, hear, touch, feel, sense, experience the power of that love in whatever way is best for us.

Those of us on the road of forgiveness are already joined by the risen Christ, even as he joined two of his disciples on the road to Emmaus. They were full of sorrow, bewilderment, anger over what had happened in the crucifixion. They were not expecting him, but he joined them anyway. They walked together to an inn for supper. He sat down with them:

> He took bread, blessed and broke it, and gave it to them. *Then their eyes were opened, and they recognized him*; . . . They said to each other, "Were not our hearts burning within us while he was talking to us on the road?" (Luke 24:30-32, italics mine)

Our eyes too will be opened as he walks with us. Our inner vision will be made pure, single. And we will see God.

~

Suggested Meditation for Focusing on God's Light

Blessed are the pure in heart,
for they will see God (Matthew 5:8).

This meditation also may come too soon for you. If you have recently moved through the meditation of mercy, you may need to stay with that one for a long time. But when you feel ready to see your wounder in yet another light, enter this meditation with a sense of awe. You are asking to see God!

Rest your body. Give thanks because God rejoices that you want to see through God's eyes. Breathe slowly and deeply a few times, and then relax into gentle breathing.

Move reflectively through some of the stages of forgiveness you have experienced already: naming the hurt, feeling the pain, opening to God's gentle power and new expectations, making clear choices, envisioning others' pain. How do you feel at this point? How does your body feel? Lay a hand gently on any bodily part that feels in any way stressed, tight, or uncomfortable.

"Come," my heart says, "seek his face!"
Your face, Lord, do I seek. (Psalm 27:8)

Lay your palms gently on your heart area, close your eyes, and sense the light of God shining in the center of your heart like a star. Think of the star quietly expanding in slow, pulsing, radiating waves throughout your body. Your whole body is being peacefully filled with the immediate presence of God's light.

Now pay attention to your breathing. Let each gentle breath be the taking in of God's breath of life. Don't gasp or push it. Let it flow into you and out from you quietly and naturally. Your body and spirit are being renewed.

Rest for a while in the envisioning or just the thought of this quiet, rhythmically pulsing light. When you feel ready, open your eyes, look at your hands, gaze at a tree, look at some colored object. Do you notice a difference in the way it looks, in the way you see it?

Think of ways to focus on God's deep, flowing, healing light throughout the day. Think of ways to breathe in and out deeply and slowly God's breath, God's air.

When you feel ready, ask God to bring to your mind some person you find it hard to like, perhaps a person who has hurt you in some way. God says to you, "Seek my face." Focus on that person, picture or just think of a star shining in that individual's heart. Picture or just think of that expanding light flowing throughout his or her body. Think of God's breathing the breath of new life into that person.

How might that person's face look when healed, renewed, made whole? How might the expression change? What new being might look at you through those eyes?

Can you draw, paint, color, or sculpt that new person of splendor in the other? What are some other ways you can celebrate that inner child of God?

If words come to you more easily than inner pictures, you can inwardly say to that person: Child of God, there is incredible beauty within you, shining beneath your hurts and barriers. Child of God, let your splendor shine forth to bless me. In the name of Jesus who sees who you really are.

When you feel ready, turn your thoughts to your own self. Think of some recent difficult situation or encounter or a difficult experience yet to come. Picture or think of or just speak to the living Christ, the Awakener, near you, welcoming your inner splendor with outstretched hand. Or you can use words: Living Christ, release my inner splendor, my inner healed child of God to bless me and those around me. In the power of your name.

How does this encounter with your inner self feel in your body, in your face, your muscles? Can you paint it, dance it? Ask for the blessing of your deep, shining self.

Stand up, stretch, open your palms, and give thanks to God. Turn again, when ready, to your daily life.

Chapter Eight

Bringing the Passionate Peace

Blessed are the peacemakers,
for they will be called children of God.
—Matthew 5:9

*G*ood night, darling. The peace of God be with you," I said to my tiny daughter many years ago as I turned out the bedroom light. Out of the darkness came a firm little voice: "I don't *want* peace! I want wild things! I want excitement!"

I laughed indulgently, went to my room, and then sat down and thought about it. What an insight my daughter had given me! We usually associate that word *peace* with mere lack of conflict, quiescence, passivity. We think of peacemakers as people who don't make waves, who calm others with soothing words. But that is not what Jesus meant by *peace* when he stood among his frightened disciples that Easter night of his resurrection and said, "Peace [the shalom] be with you" (John 20:19).

The word *shalom* does not mean merely the opposite of conflict. It means wholeness, well-being, a deep and energized harmony of body and soul. It implies a close relationship of blessedness and healing with God. We don't really have the word's equivalent in English.

The shalom is really what is meant when Jesus in the Sermon on the Mount told his followers, "Be perfect, therefore, as your heavenly Father is perfect" (Matthew 5:48). This translation has been so misunderstood and has led to so much anguished compulsiveness about not making mistakes. "Be perfect" did not mean never making mistakes. Read that verse in context. Jesus was talking about the love that radiates to everyone, enemy as well as friend. "Be perfect" is better translated as "be a whole person," so held and healed in God's shalom that one is enabled to love in this way.

My little girl was quite right. When Jesus brings us God's shalom, we are not invited to passivity. We are challenged, to use my child's words, to "all kinds of excitement," to the adventures, the risk taking, of love.

God's shalom includes all kinds of people. It is a love that is a dance of opposites, a passionate meeting of polarities who have not polarized. Shalom is expressed in Isaiah's vision often called "the peaceable kingdom":

The wolf shall live with the lamb,
    the leopard shall lie down with the kid. . . .
The cow and the bear shall graze,

their young shall lie down together; . . .
The nursing child shall play over the hole of the asp, . . .
They will not hurt or destroy
on all my holy mountain. (Isaiah 11:6-9)

And just how is this love affair between these wild opposites made possible? We are told, "For the earth will be full of the knowledge of the Lord as the waters cover the sea" (verse 9).

In scripture, to know someone, to have knowledge of the person, did not refer to intellectual understanding. It meant an intimate relationship, a deep union. When we are in deep and growing union with God we begin to exult in the differences of others, just as God exults in the uniqueness of each of us. When we are in intimate relationship with God, we long passionately for the other person's fulfillment in every way just as God longs for the healing and fulfillment of each of us.

In the same spirit of adventure, God invites us to encounter the opposites within *ourselves*: the introvert–the extrovert, the giver–the receiver, the assertive–the gentle, the one who acts–the one who reflects, and so forth. We are challenged not to make a melting pot of our inner opposites but to help them learn to live together in God's shalom, the passionate peace.

The person who brings the shalom, that vibrant, energized wholeness, brings this peace not only between the outer and inner contrasts but also to the deepest blocks within. I experienced an enormous spiritual and emotional transition some years ago when I realized that my deepest faults when healed became my greatest gifts. For example, when our tendency to anger and irritability is healed, this energy originally expressed as anger may become a powerful energy for justice. When our anxiety and worry are healed, we may discover that this energy is intended to be sensitivity, a healing empathy toward others.[1]

Instead of asking God to kill our destructive energies, how much more powerful to ask God to heal and transform them. Otherwise we are constantly warring with ourselves. Forgiving ourselves in this way makes a radical difference in our lives and personalities.

As I reflected on this transformation one day, I suddenly received an insight into these puzzling words:

> Come to terms quickly with your accuser while you are on the way to court with him, or your accuser may hand you over to the judge, and the judge to the guard, and you will be thrown into prison. Truly I tell you, you will never get out until you have paid the last penny. (Matthew 5:25-26)

What in the world is *that* all about? I used to ask myself. Why in the middle of the great sermon is Jesus suddenly advising his followers how to avoid arrest and lawsuits? I studied the context of the verses. In the verses preceding and following, Jesus is talking about the inner righteousness of the heart: Murder is evil, yes, but inappropriate anger and verbal abuse are also evil as ways of emotional murder. Giving gifts at God's altar is useless if there is unhealed rancor in the heart. Outward fidelity in marriage is only a cracked shell if one is constantly lusting for and violating others in thoughts and heart. So who is this "accuser" who is trying to take us to judgment and to jail? Surely it is our *self-hatred*, which is as dangerous as hating others. It is our self-contempt that would hold us in inner prisons until we have "paid up" for every wrong thing we have ever done or thought.

If we allow this inner judge to have control over us, we begin a life of anxious contrivance trying to earn God's love and the love of others. Then we begin to treat others in the same way. We hold both friends and enemies in a book of balances, adding up merits and demerits with a keen, judgmental eye for every slight imbalance.

This legalistic attitude can be expressed in small ways: "I did him a favor, now he owes me"; "She called her two times last week, but phoned me only once"; or in more threatening ways: "life for life, eye for eye, tooth for tooth, hand for hand, foot for foot, burn for burn, wound for wound" (Exodus 21:23-25).

When Peter asked Jesus if he should forgive others as many as seven times, Jesus answered, "not seven times, but, I tell you, seventy-seven times" (Matthew 18:22). Obviously he was not saying mark off each forgiveness up to seventy-seven and then stop forgiving. *He was wiping out all calculated response* both to ourselves and to others. He threw a legalism of checks and balances out the window. He invited us to a wider place, a freer air, where compassion and mercy are no longer a matter of arithmetic.

But until we let God release *us*, we cannot release ourselves or others. We remain in that condition of self-judgment, a judgment of others, that spiritual prison, anxiously counting up those pennies! God longs to enter these prisons of ours, throw open the doors, bring us into what theologians call *grace*—the realm of free gifting—not to earn love but *because* we are already loved.

Therefore in my healing journey toward myself I do try to "come to terms quickly" with my inner accuser before I get to the point of rigid self-judgment. I try to ask the inner accuser, What are you trying to tell me? Have I wounded another? Have I wounded myself? Are you something that is hurting within me? What is your name? What is your need?

Listening to our inner selves with respectful attention releases us from rigid judgment. It opens the door to God's healing and transformation within. Likewise it prepares the way for empathetic listening to others, perceiving the wound, helping to release the gift. Bringing this inner shalom both to ourselves and to others is one of the supreme adventures on the journey of forgiveness.

One of the deepest concerns of the shalom bringer is discovering ways to keep from passing on the pain that is received to others or even more importantly, ways to pass the power of loving release to one another. How can we do this throughout the day? How can we do this throughout the generations?

As an example, if I quarrel with my spouse in the morning and hurt is given and received, I am much more likely to drive carelessly and rudely on the way to work. Another driver, seething with outrage over my rudeness, will exhibit more road-rage to other drivers. Some of those drivers will unload their irritation on colleagues or customers at work. They, in turn, will project their frustration and anger onto their families that evening. By the end of the day, perhaps more than a hundred people have been infected by my unhealed anger more quickly than they would have caught the flu!

The person who brings God's shalom becomes keenly aware of this dangerous cycle of emotional infection. At the very moment of assault by someone else's projected pain, the shalom bringer will enter the forgiveness process, admitting the painful impact, asking for God's help, trying to understand what may have hurt the assaulter, and then with firm intentionality make the choice not to pass the pain and anger on to the next person. Thus the destructive cycle is broken.

With generational pain, the peacemaker resolves that the abuse passed from parent to child, perhaps for more than a hundred years, will stop with him or her. The peacemaker will ask God and other people for help and healing, will learn how to forgive and to release others, including individuals of past generations.

For example, a woman told me she had evidence that a great-grandfather in her family had been a child molester. She had not been a victim, but she knew others who were, and the situation had affected the whole family destructively for decades. She was not excusing this man's behavior, though she knew he probably was acting out of his own childhood wounds, but she did feel guided to enter into intercessory prayer for the whole family, including the great-grandfather who had died some years earlier.

She envisioned the whole family standing in a circle around the great-grandfather. Christ the Healer (she sensed his presence in the form of a woman) went to each family member, surrounding each with the light of healing and special blessing and then surrounding the whole family with the light of protection. Then she envisioned the family members raising their hands toward the great-grandfather, praying for his healing. She sensed a silver-white light forming around his feet, slowly rising up through his body. At the end of the meditation she felt a change within herself and also sensed a change in the communal body of her family.

There are many ways to pray for former generations. Some people look at family albums and pray for those pictured there. Others may draw a family tree, asking the risen Jesus to heal the wounded parts of the tree. Others will want to write a prayer or draw or sculpt a figure symbolizing the whole family.

Before praying for the pain of generations, we should listen to our inner guidance as to whether we are ready to enter into this form of intercession. Some of us may need first to focus on our own healing for a long time. We also must be careful never to push or even urge other people to enter into this way of praying. Many people are still too tangled in their pain to pray this way safely until their own healing has deepened. When generational healing prayers are suggested, participants should be cautioned to move into some other form of prayer if they feel increasing anxiety or anger. Praying for the healing of generational, historical pain may produce less fear and be more effective if we join with a group of others involved with that history.

Shalom bringers will not only seek to break the destructive cycles of passed-on pain, will not only seek to heal the wounds of the past, but they will also deliberately start a cycle of love and celebration of one another. To speak honest praise to another person is as infectious as passing on hurt.

I think we humans are literally *starving* for healthy praise. Praising another is not flattery, bribery, or propitiation.

Honest praise is keen awareness and celebration of the shining aspects of another person. Many parents hesitate to praise their child, fearful of making the child complacent and self-satisfied. On the contrary, sincere praise is the best possible foundation and encouragement for growth.

Both scripture and our liturgies urge us to open our mouths and give praise to God. Do we ever stop to ask ourselves *why* God wants us to do that? Does God, like a rock star, need applause in order to keep going? Hardly. God asks us to give praise so that we may learn how to do it; so that we may learn how to open our hearts, open our mouths, and express delighted appreciation for the whole universe, including ourselves.

When we praise God, it draws us closer into a delighted relationship with God. When we give honest praise to our spouse, our friend, our child, it opens both *our* heart and that of the other. However, it may take the other a while to get used to it, so begin in simple, small ways. I remember reading a book years ago, a daily-diary type of autobiography, in which the wife describes one of those delightful conversations when she and her husband found themselves beginning almost each sentence with "Well, one thing I like about you is . . . ."

Giving and receiving (for *receiving* praise is every bit as important as the giving and may take more practice) begin to open a locked door within us, begin to melt a repressed core, begin to let loose new springs of life-giving water within us and among us. Praise opens us up!

God too delights to praise *us*. I love what Brennan Manning wrote:

A fellow Franciscan once challenged me: "Do you ever reflect upon the fact that Jesus feels proud of you? Proud that you accepted the faith which he offered you? Proud that you chose him for a friend and Lord? Is proud of you that you haven't given up? . . . Proud that you trust that he can help you? . . . grateful to you for pausing to smile, comfort? . . . Do you ever think of Jesus being grateful to you for learning more about him so that you can speak to others more deeply and truly about him?"[2]

Of course, it is not only words that bring the shalom. Deeper than words is what we radiate just by our presence. One may bring peace also by redemptive action with others.

I was talking with a clergyman about a fragmenting conflict between him and other members of his ethnic group within his church and neighborhood. They were deeply divided on a number of issues, and this division had led to a cold, unspoken hostility. My minister friend told me he had called a meeting with others of his community, all of whom were Christian.

"Will you sit down and talk things through?" I asked. "Will you talk about the hurts you all feel and ways to heal them?"

"No," he answered thoughtfully. "Not at this point. I don't feel we are ready for talking things over. I feel instead that we should celebrate the Eucharist together. Then perhaps we can plan things we can do for the poor in our city, for the delinquent teenagers or the homeless. There is a lot of healing in loving, active service together. But the main thing will be to celebrate the Eucharist together, first thing, each time we meet."

I learned something important from this friend. When fellow Christians are deeply divided on issues, if they center around the risen Christ with prayer, both verbal and silent, and celebrate the Eucharist together, the living presence of the Christ brings healing answers far deeper than we had dreamed.

In all these various ways, the peacemaker, the bringer of God's shalom, enters into profound intercession. Intercession means an interlinking, a remaking of connections between parts that have been separated. When we have been relinked with God and others, our newborn selves weave new interlinkings of love, just by existing. These interlinkings affect not only those whom we see but also those whom we may never see in this life. I believe intercession also affects those who have gone through the transition of death, helping them as they increasingly unfold within God.

The shalom bringers spread a sense of warmth, comfort, hope, and well-being even before a word is spoken. They themselves are the interlinking, not just their words and actions. They do not talk about religion all the time. They are not constantly telling us to cheer up and look on the bright side. They may not say anything special at all, but when we are with them we feel understood, accepted, welcomed.

When we think of these men and women in our lives, we feel as if God is reaching out to us through them. We know that if God is like them—only much more so—then the universe is in safe hands. The glory of God shines through their faces and touches us through their hands.

We call them the children of God.

~

Suggested Meditation for the Peace Bringers

Blessed are the peacemakers,
for they will be called children of God (Matthew 5:9).

Bring your body into a peaceful posture: curl up, lie or sit with good support, or take a slow walk.

Focus on your breathing, and let it become calm, slow, gentle. Notice how your body is feeling. Does your body feel well balanced and at peace with itself? Lay a gentle hand on any bodily parts that feel stressed. Think of any bodily part you may have neglected or overworked recently: eyes, arms, hands, feet, back, legs. Touch them with love, and thank them for their faithful work for your good.

Reflect on the meaning of shalom, the biblical word for peace. It means well-being, wholeness, vitality that is balanced through one's soul and body, a unity and harmony between body and soul.

When you feel ready, think of two inner opposites, such as the active organizer and the quiet contemplative. Bring them together in God's presence upon your own holy mountain. How do they look? How do they react toward each other: with discomfort or each ignoring the other or each vying for control? Do they seem to honor each other and value each other?

Ask these two parts of yourself to talk together about their places in your life. Can they bring enriched unity to your life, rather than disunion? What does each one offer that the other one needs?

Is there an inner part of you that is a condemning judge? Let the living Christ invite this one to come forth. Listen to what this "judge" has to say, knowing you are protected by the Christ who came not to judge us or condemn us but to bring us life. What is the true face of the inner judge? Is it a wounded, frightened part of yourself? Is it hiding under the mask of an accuser? Does it accuse because it fears being accused?

Ask Christ the Healer to reach out to the frightened inner one who hides under the role of accuser and the robes of a condemning judge. What is its real fear and hurt? Can you envision Christ laying healing hands on this inner one? Do you sense any change in your body at this point?

Rest and reflect quietly. When you feel ready, ask the Christ to invite forth some beautiful, radiant part of yourself: your ability to love and give; your gift of listening and comforting; your gift of observation and discernment; your gift for laughter and delight; your gift of leadership and creativity; your ability to wonder, to explore, to learn; whatever part of yourself that has given help and joy and healing to others. This beautiful splendor within you has brought joy to God. God not only has compassion on you but also delights in you. Receive this joy from God. Let yourself also become joyful that you have beautiful things within you.

You may want to draw, color, sculpt, or dance what you feel about your inner selves: your exciting contrasts, your hidden ones, your inner splendor.

As God's peace, God's shalom, brings you together in inner balance and harmony, how does your body feel?

As you are gathered together in love, how do you feel you can learn to respond to the complexities, the opposites, the wounded, frightened ones, the glorious ones in the people around you? Do you sense a difference beginning?

As you gradually come forth from your meditation, you may want to hug yourself in celebration. Lightly rub your face, hands, arms, wrists, giving thanks to God for the complexity and unity in your bodily self.

CHAPTER NINE

Living As Whole Persons among the Unreconciled

Blessed are those who are persecuted
for righteousness' sake,
for theirs is the kingdom of heaven.

—Matthew 5:10

*J*esus harbored no illusions. He knew that though our new released life in God's shalom would draw to us many surprising new friends, so would our new life raise up some surprising enemies. He told us that sometimes "one's foes will be members of one's own household" (Matthew 10:36).

This warning does not necessarily mean that an enemy will dislike us or wish us harm. An enemy may think he or she loves us, and may wish us well, but in fact stand against not only our way of life but also against the person we have become. The word *hate,* for example, does not mean necessarily the same as *dislike.* The roots of that word mean to turn away totally from something or someone. Many an enemy may feel he or she is acting for our good by resisting and rejecting who we are and what we stand for.

"I have left my former church," a young man told me. "That church is a strict, rigid group, and I realize now it has made me unhappy all my life. But it took me a long time to make my decision, and it wasn't easy, for after all I was born and brought up in the church. I have a whole new attitude toward God now. I feel so free and loved. I can even love myself, which I was not allowed to do before. The church's whole emphasis was on sin and unworthiness and guilt.

"But my parents just can't take [my leaving the church]. They think my soul is lost. They think their way is the only way to salvation and God's favor. Every day they phone and argue. They've gotten other members to phone and argue. They have told me that I won't be welcome back home as their son unless I repent and return."

"It's strange," a middle-aged man mused, "my wife is much less close to me now that I feel so much more peaceful and relaxed and have been able to forgive that coworker of mine. She doesn't like my praying for people instead of yelling at them. I think she believes I'm trying to push her into religion."

I heard a similar story later. "I've gone back to my husband after a long separation," a young woman shared. "We had counseling and worked out a better life together, and we are happy in our new life. But my coworkers at my job now like me *less*! They used to be so sweet and understanding when I would come in crying and tired after a sleepless night. But now they're not natural with me. They don't include me when they go out together. I see them whispering to each other and then suddenly stopping when I come into the room."

"There's been a big change in my life," a middle-aged woman told me. "I am really trying to grow spiritually and loving it. I read a lot of books about it, and I go to retreats and am learning so much. I would love to tell my husband about it, but he just shrugs it off and refuses to discuss the change in me. Either he ignores my new life, or he makes condescending remarks about the books I read and the people I'm seeing. And whenever I'm trying to get to a group meeting, he always brings something up that he thinks I ought to be doing instead. He's not hostile exactly; he just stonewalls the whole thing. I'm really not trying to make *him* change, but I'd love to share what's happening to me."

When our lives have changed, when we have experienced inner healing and release, many people who had been close to us before now will feel upset and threatened by the change in us. They may feel that we don't need them anymore. They may feel some bitterness and envy that we are happy while they still suffer. They may believe we think ourselves superior or that we are judging them or trying to push them where they don't want to go. They may feel they are losing us and wish we would go back to our former condition of neediness. Sometimes they feel an inner urging also to change, and that feels threatening.

Sometimes people around us genuinely disapprove of changes within us, especially if we have left a former church, community, belief, or ideology in which they still believe. For what they consider to be our own good, they try to pull us back, set up obstacles in our way, withdraw approval. Can this be called persecution?

I believe that any attempt to make our spiritual path harder for us, any attempt to make us suffer for what we believe is right, any attempt to manipulate or tempt us to a way we do not wish to go is indeed persecution. We should not expect enemies at every turn, of course, or go around with a piously martyred attitude. We do need to be aware of what can and often does happen when we undertake a new way of living.

Persecution can take many forms:

Stonewalling. Refusal to discuss, talk seriously, respond to real changes in our lives.

Hostility. Assuming the worst of our motives; accusations; anger.

Ostracizing. Distancing—the silent treatment; withdrawal from physical or emotional closeness; exclusion from formerly shared activities.

Obstructing. Creating problems and stumbling blocks; sabotaging in subtle or overt ways; making difficulties.

Threatening. Creating fear that we will be abandoned; that others will be turned against us; that we will lose our job, status, or reputation.

Demeaning. Trivializing, ridiculing, teasing, gossiping, showing contempt.

Tempting. Manipulating, using our weaknesses against us, holding out various rewards for submission.

Disempowering. Creating doubt within us that we can

maintain our new life; raising fears about our worthiness, competence, strength.

Negativity. Predicting failure and loss.

Arguing. Debating constantly, nagging, pushing.

Group pressure. Gathering others to demean, negate, obstruct, and argue.

I have read that modern forms of persecution are less like being eaten by lions than nibbled to death by ducks!

I hope someday someone will write a book called *And the Next Day . . .* based on the healings by Jesus. How did the community of the woman taken in adultery react when she was saved by Jesus from the stoning and forgiven by him (John 8:3-11)? How did the neighbors react when Jesus healed the bent woman on the Sabbath (Luke 13:10-17)? What happened as time went on after Jesus healed the man possessed by demons and sent him back to his community (Mark 5:1-20)? Was Lazarus able to live a normal life in Bethany after Jesus raised him from the dead (John 11:38-44)? How about the younger son in the prodigal son story? What happened between him and his brother, beginning not only the next day but that evening (Luke 15:11-32)?

We know there were many rejoicing, welcoming friends in these stories, but we know that there must have been others who found the healed ones uncomfortable to live with, who felt threatened by what they represented, who felt envy because the healed were shown such favor, who felt too many rules were being broken by all this spontaneity and freedom, who felt unneeded and wished the healed one was back where he or she used to be, who felt left out, suspicious, scared, hostile.

Peter began to say to him, "Look, we have left every-thing and followed you." Jesus said, "Truly I tell you, there is no one who has left house or brothers or sisters or mother or father or children or fields, for my sake and for the sake of the good news, who will not receive a hundredfold now in this age—houses, brothers and sisters, mothers and children, and fields with persecu-tions—and in the age to come eternal life." (Mark 10:28-30)

This passage has always fascinated me! Jesus speaks (in metaphors) of the overflowing abundance of blessings each one of us who joins our life to him will receive. Each of us will be healed, released, and empowered by him. Along with the abundance and blessings of our inner life, we will receive (he seems to add this almost casually) *persecutions*! Is he merely saying that nothing is perfect, or is he actually saying that per-secutions along with the fields actually are *part of* the blessing?

How can persecutions be part of blessedness? The reason given is significant: "for theirs is the kingdom of heaven." We have come full circle. This phrase concludes the very first beatitude for those who are "poor in spirit," which means those who know their need of God. We need that total dependence the most keenly when we experience the perse-cutions, in whatever form. It is then we need "the kingdom and the power and the glory," which enfold us, empower us, as we pray to be delivered from evil.

I had a strange experience on a city bus some years ago. It was a long ride through some of the worst areas of a large city, and the bus was full. A man got on, looked around and seemed to recognize a young woman seated across from me. He squeezed in next to her and began to whisper something to her. She ignored him, turned her head away, but I could see that she was turning very pale and looked frightened. His voice got louder and he began to curse her fiercely as she shrank away. Evil seemed to fill the bus like clouds of poison gas. The driver stopped the bus and called the police, but by now the man was out of control, snarling and yelling threats. Suddenly words filled my mind: "In the name, through the power, and by the word of Jesus Christ, I surround us all with God's wall of protecting fire, and I thank God that this is done." (Someone had given me that prayer years earlier for emergencies.) I *felt* as if I had stood up and pronounced these words of strong protection very loudly, but in fact I don't think I had moved or spoken aloud, for no one was looking at me. Nevertheless, the words *were* pronounced whether by me or through me, whether aloud or silently, for I could feel their reverberation throughout the bus.

Instantly something or some*one* else filled that bus. It is hard to describe what I sensed, but it felt as if huge presences entered the bus and walked up and down the aisle. I could not see them, but they were enormous and filled with light and indescribable power. The man immediately fell silent, looked confused, went to the back of the bus, and sat down quietly. I crossed the aisle and sat next to the young woman who was trembling violently, and I tried to soothe her. The police arrived a few minutes later, and the man went with them meekly, still looking dazed.

The power of that experience is vivid in my memory. I don't think I had ever used that prayer before, certainly not in a situation of such potential danger. That bus route had been the scene of several knife fights and shootings. But I felt as if the vast presences there were concerned far more with the evil present than with mere physical danger. We are not always promised physical safety, but Jesus told us to pray, "deliver us from evil" (Matthew 6:13, RSV). Evil is a spiritual, devastating threat to our *whole* self and those around us. The night before his death, Jesus prayed for his disciples (and for all of us who love him in the ages to come):

> Holy Father, protect them in your name that you have given me . . . I am not asking you to take them out of the world, but I ask you to protect them from evil. (John 17:11, 15, alt. trans.)

I was moved by John Mogabgab's reflection on the Book of Daniel's story of the three Israelites sentenced to death in a fiery furnace in Babylon. As the amazed King Nebuchadnezzar watches the three men surviving in the midst of the flames, he observes yet another mystery:

> "But I see four men unbound, walking in the middle of the fire, and they are not hurt; and *the fourth has the appearance of a god*" (Daniel 3:25, italics mine). . . . The church has long seen the mysterious fourth man in this remarkable story as a figure of Christ. . . . Silently, unobtrusively, in the swaddled child of Bethlehem, God enters the all-consuming furnace of a fallen world. It glows with the terrible intensity of sorrow, guilt, and self-hatred. It shudders with the blistering violence of ancient animosities. . . . Who is this unexpected

visitor moving among us, and how is it that those with him seem not to be devoured by the evil that oppresses our days?[1]

The early martyrs believed literally that when they faced torture or execution, the risen Jesus Christ was fully within them, body and soul, taking upon himself the impact of their pain and shielding them from the even worse impact of the hatred and evil that surrounded them. He did not leave them there to struggle alone with pain and evil. They lived in, walked in, and if necessary died in the living embrace of the kingdom, the power, and the glory.

We do not need to be in flames, facing lions, or even on a dangerous bus ride to be clasped and lifted up by this luminous power. In the midst of any challenge, suffering, hostility—no matter how minor it seems in comparison to the world's vast suffering—we can claim what God has promised, the presence of God's empowered love through Jesus Christ.

When we ask for the gift of self-forgiveness, sometimes we feel we do not deserve this immediate presence of the living God. After all, we ourselves have persecuted others, whether in major or minor ways. If we are experiencing hurt because others will not forgive us, even if we have asked forgiveness, don't we deserve that pain? Who are we to ask for God's deliverance?

It is true that we have no right to demand the forgiveness of those whom we have injured. Nor have we the right to insist on reconciliation. If reconciliation comes as a grace of healing, we accept it with joy and gratitude. But if another person remains hostile and suspicious toward us, God helps us to accept it while continuing in prayer for the healing of the other.

Whether forgiveness is given or not by the other person, we are *still* welcomed by God to the dignity and blessedness of the children of God. Though we remain responsible for our hurtful acts, the burden is lifted, we are out of the prison, we have entered a new creation.

We can say with Paul the Apostle, as he reflected on his history as a persecutor:

> I am grateful to Christ Jesus our Lord, who has strengthened me, because he judged me faithful and appointed me to his service, even though I was formerly a blasphemer, a persecutor, and a man of violence. But I received mercy because I had acted ignorantly in unbelief, and the grace of our Lord overflowed for me with the faith and love that are in Christ Jesus. (1 Timothy 1:12-14)

Whether wounded or former wounder, we can search the scriptures and find the great symbols of spiritual protection and shelter for times of threat, stress, challenge, disempowerment. Just this morning a young woman pastor told me that when she feels most vulnerable, open to hurt, she is given the inner image of a strong but translucent shell, shaped like praying hands or a Gothic arch, folding around her. This image does not mean she withdraws from love, for she is a warm, loving person. It is her sign of shelter.

For myself, I ask the living, healing Jesus Christ to stand between me and a person who may hurt or drain me, ministering to that person in the way he or she most needs. I do not feel separated from the other person, but I know that the Christ, not I, is the source of life, the healing fountain for all of us. I sense then the tendrils of need and hunger going into the heart of the Christ who can comfort and feed. This is not only a picture prayer for the needs of the other person but also a prayer of shelter for me, so that I will not be drained or invaded by the need of the other.

These forms of protection in stress and with stressful people do not distance us or repress the flow of love. Rather they release the flow of love because we are not subconsciously always trying to defend ourselves in every encounter or helplessly surrendering to every invasive or draining interaction.

When we are invited, challenged, by Christ to join him on the healing frontiers of this dangerous world, we are not expected to enter these risks alone. Always we are meant to be as those deeply abiding in the living vine or—to change the metaphor—surrounded and strengthened by that mighty Heart.

> He is now living, a Presence, a Personality, yet a Being so infinite in power that He can go through the doors of our bodies and enter into us and abide in us—a Being so great that the light of His presence can shine like the sun on millions of people and yet not be diminished. . . . Words are not great enough to describe that sense of walking about in a body of light that is not our own, but is His light.[2]

～

Suggested Meditation for Persecution Experiences

Blessed are those who are persecuted
for righteousness' sake, for theirs is the kingdom
of heaven (Matthew 5:10).

Make yourself especially comfortable for this meditation. Enter into slow, deep breathing for a few seconds and then let your breath become light and natural.

For several minutes just rest in God's presence, in whatever way you feel closest to God. Let the weight of your body and any weight on your heart rest totally on God's strength.

This is a meditation on spiritual protection when we feel threatened or disempowered in any way as we try to live as whole, loving persons.

What are of protection are helpful for you? Scripture suggests God's strong hands, God's wings sheltering and covering you, the powerful presence of Jesus, vast angels of light around you, your own inner sanctuary, a circle of light, a cloak of light, a powerful spoken invocation, Jesus' name, the name of the Trinity, a special bodily stance or posture, a strong rock lifting you up. All of these metaphors are biblical, and there are many others found in scripture. Other images may come to you inwardly.

Which image, word, or thought seems the right one for you now? Rest in this powerful protection of God. Breathe its air. Sense the vastness of its strength. This is the very power of God's kingdom, God's sovereign realm.

Now begin to envision or just think of how that strength not only surrounds and enfolds you but also enters your inner heart, the very cells of your body. It shines through you and radiates to others.

When ready, think of some person or group that tries to pull you back to your old life, to block your way, or to drain away your power. It may be someone you have to encounter often. Envision yourself together with this person. You are compassionately aware of that person's own inner fears and hurts, but you know you need protection. You are surrounded by your own special God-given image of strength or the special word or prayer God gives you. Nothing can destroy, disempower, or drain away "the kingdom and the power and the glory" that both surround and permeate you.

Within your protection, envision or just ask the living Jesus Christ, the Healer, to come to the other person, laying healing hands on her or his fear, hurt, or anger.

When you feel ready, give thanks to God for the love that surrounds you and the other person.

Breathe slowly and deeply three or four times. Lightly massage your face and your hands, and come back to your daily life.

> I arise today through the strength of heaven:
>> light of the sun, radiance of moon,
>> splendor of fire, speed of lightning,
>> swiftness of wind, depth of sea,
>> stability of earth, firmness of rock.

Forgiveness

I arise today through God's strength to pilot me . . .
God's word to speak for me,
God's hand to guard me,
God's way to lie before me.

I summon all these powers between me and every power
that may oppose my body and soul.

—Attributed to Saint Patrick, 500 C.E.

CHAPTER TEN

Becoming a Singing, Shining Enemy

Blessed are you when people revile you and persecute you and utter all kinds of evil against you falsely on my account. Rejoice and be glad, for your reward is great in heaven.
—Matthew 5:11-12

When I was thirteen years old, a dog ran under my bicycle as I was riding swiftly downhill. I fell and both broke and dislocated bones in my hand and was badly scratched and gouged. I had never had an accident before and was terrified at the thought of bone setting, stitches, tetanus shots.

When the doctor left the office for a few moments before treatment began, my mother, who knew me well, turned to me, took my unbroken hand in hers, and said, "Darling, this is a great and important moment for you. You have a choice to make now, and it will influence you the rest of your life. You can crumple in tears, hang back, stiffen, and resist everything the doctor tries to do for you, or you can choose to take it in high gear, like our car heading up a steep hill." (She was a marvelous driver and had recently explained the gearshift to me.) "I mean you can choose now whether you will move forward with courage and most of all, a high heart!"

Somehow the fear at that moment dropped away from me. I knew I had a choice. I was not a victim anymore. Somehow she not only had pulled me out of a pit of fear but literally had called forth the power that was in me. I began to feel almost excited! During the painful proceedings that followed, I glanced at her once or twice, and she smiled and formed the words silently with her lips, "Take it in high, darling." Though she died over twenty-five years ago, I can still inwardly hear her saying those words when I face a scary challenge in a timid, grudging spirit, dragging my feet, "Take it in *high*, darling!" Paul drew forth the same high spirit for his young assistant Timothy who was chosen for dangerous, difficult work and travels for the early church: "For the spirit that God gave us is no craven spirit, but one to inspire strength, love, and self-discipline" (2 Timothy 1:7, NEB).

These last four great blessings are a final, triumphant unfolding and progression: the pure in heart will see God; the peacemakers will become the children of God; the persecuted will receive the kingdom of God's heaven; and, those who are reviled falsely by their enemies will enter into the joy of that heaven. To me, these are not just promises for the future but a present reality beginning, if we choose, this moment.

Becoming a Singing, Shining Enemy

This final blessing, as with the preceding one, focuses on our life with the hostile and unreconciled, but it takes us further into the strength that not only endures but also *sings.* This high-heartedness is a distinguishing sign of those who are rooted and grounded in Christ as their singing strength. The living Christ calls forth in us that spirit of adventure and courageous joy the way my mother called it forth from me so long ago.

Within our journey of forgiveness, release, and love's new creation, wonderful companions will be given us, but sometimes we will also be considered an enemy. An enemy, as explained in the preceding chapter, is not necessarily someone evil or even someone who dislikes us. An enemy is someone who blocks our way, who considers us or what we stand for as detrimental to his or her beliefs.

Judas probably had concluded that Jesus was detrimental to the hopes and expectations of the Zealots and was therefore an enemy. The Roman Empire legally declared the Christians "enemies of the state"; everything the church stood for threatened Roman values. Some of the most upright, idealistic of the emperors (such as Marcus Aurelius) were among the most zealous persecutors of Christians just because they cared so deeply for what they thought was good for Rome and its people.

Such zealots occasionally may be found in our lives still. Often they are good people, sincere people, trying to do what they consider best for their community. Some years ago a devout church member became outraged by an article I had written for a church magazine. She persuaded her minister to throw out every copy of that month's issue so that none of the other members of her church, at least, would be exposed to such dangerous teaching. Then she wrote to the magazine's editor, asking him for my address so that she could write and tell me how to become a Christian. With utmost sincerity she believed I was a danger to true Christian teaching, an enemy.

Recently a Christian denomination published a list of religious authors considered to be dangerous heretics. Among those listed were some of our finest, most Christ-centered teachers, ministers, and priests. I am sorry to say I was not on the list! I would have been in the best of company!

In every church, every political party in every nation, every ethnic group, workplace, corporation, and family, there are those who look upon people pushing back frontiers with new ideas and alternative viewpoints or asking questions as dangerous people who should be suppressed, as enemies.

People who are frightened by the thought of freedom, who feel threatened by our own release, may see us as enemies. Those who are too proud to ask for help may reject the outstretched helping hand as if it were an enemy. Those who take on leadership positions to help work through communal problems can quickly become targets for enmity, blame, and criticism. And, as pointed out earlier, even when we have asked forgiveness of another and tried to make restitution, the other may still look upon us as an enemy.

Jesus was realistic about such reactions. He knew that not only would we have enemies, but we often would be regarded as enemies. The real question is, What kind of enemy will we be? the usual kind? an enemy who says hurtful things because we have been hurt? one who becomes bitter? one who sinks into despair? one who becomes cynical about justice? one who withdraws from the action vowing never to stick our neck out again? one who endures bravely but with grim heaviness of spirit? one who has lost joy and laughter within the persecution?

There is another way of being an enemy. As a child I was fascinated to read the true story of a battle a thousand years ago. As the army advanced, a famous knight galloped in front of the ranks. He was renowned not only as a fearless fighter but as a singer, a poet. As he rode ahead of the army toward the enemy, he *sang*. As he sang, he tossed up his sword where it circled glittering in the sunshine, caught it by its hilt, and tossed it again, still singing. There was not only courage that battle morning; there was laughter and song as the army advanced. Whatever we choose to do on this journey of forgiveness, let us "take it in high!"

Recently I read some ancient eyewitness accounts of the trials and deaths of early Christian martyrs. It quickly became apparent that they were not helpless victims. They chose in freedom to die rather than burn incense to pagan gods. They named their deaths by wild animals in the arenas "fighting with the beasts." Their joy went far beyond mere courage:

> The day of their victory dawned, and they marched from the prison to the amphitheatre joyfully . . . with calm faces, trembling, if at all, with joy rather than fear. Perpetua went along with shining countenance and calm step, as the beloved of God, as a wife of Christ, putting down everyone's stare by her own intense gaze.[1]

As we read such accounts, we realize we are seeing much more than endurance or even forgiveness here. We are seeing the release of an incredible joyful energy that does not merely stand but *leaps* directly into the realms of cruelty, despair, and death. It leaps, enclosed by God's heart, not to destroy but to heal, to transform.

"You are Peter, and on this rock I will build my church," said Jesus to Simon Peter (Matthew 16:18). I had always envisioned this as the rock-strengthened church standing firm against all the onslaughts and batterings of hell's forces. "Not so," a scientist who was also a lay minister once told me, "*I* see that rock of the church *not* standing still, waiting to be attacked, but thrown by God, flying through the air, crashing into the gates of evil to release those trapped there." What an insight! The risen, living Christ never could endure leaving "the spirits in prison" (1 Peter 3:19).

In the Eucharistic service we are told that the Lord Jesus, on the very night of his betrayal, took the bread, broke it, and gave it. Then he took the cup of wine, poured it, gave it, promising that he would drink the new wine with them (and us) within the realm of God. Wherever he is, that is the realm. So he drinks it with us now.

In the deepness of that night, in the pit of the betrayal, at that moment when Jesus lifted the cup, he *leaped*, along with all of us who love him, into those vast, cold prisons of the night. Those locked gates could not prevail against him. Then he went out, singing: "When they had sung the hymn, they went out to the Mount of Olives" (Mark 14:26).

And Throughout all Eternity
I forgive you, you forgive me.
As our dear Redeemer said:
"This the Wine, and this the Bread."

        —William Blake (1757-1827), "Broken Love"[2]

~

Suggested Meditation for Joy in the Midst of Stress

Blessed are you when people revile you and
persecute you . . . on my account.
Rejoice and be glad (Matthew 5:11-12).

In this meditation you may wish to sit with straight spine. At some point you may feel it natural to stand up and stretch your arms. You may want to listen to some favorite music.

Breathe slowly and deeply a few times, then relax into gentle, natural breath. Move your attention gently through your body to see if there are any bodily areas in pain, stress, tightness. Sense or picture God's warm, healing light flowing into these tight, stressed areas.

Note if any part of your body feels vulnerable, powerless, open to emotional or verbal attack. Sense or picture God's strength covering and permeating these areas.

As in the previous meditation, claim and let yourself be enfolded by your inner image of God's protecting power or the special words of shining protection.

Ask for God's joy, that special joy Jesus felt the night of the Last Supper shared with his friends. Does the joy have a special color? a shape or form of its own? Do you see an inner picture or symbol? Does it come as a word? Does it feel like a bodily posture?

Think of being at the supper, sitting at the table with Jesus and his friends. Also invite someone dear to you to sit at that table. Likewise invite one or two people who have hurt you or made the way harder for you. Let them also sit at Jesus' table. Jesus looks around the table with joyful welcome to all. Then he breaks the bread into pieces and the plate goes around the table, each serving the other. Who is sitting next to you? Can you receive the bread from your friend and give bread to the one who hurt you? (If you cannot do this yet, do not force yourself. You can return to this bread and wine as often as you wish. It may be enough for now that you are sitting at the same table.)

Then Jesus stands, lifts the cup of wine, and says, "I will drink new wine with you in God's kingdom. Drink from it, all of you here at this table. Drink it with my blessing." The cup goes around the table, each drinking from it. Are you able to take the cup from the hand of the one who hurt you and drink from it? (Again, do not force this. You may return to this table at any time.)

You are all together at the same table. Jesus says, "Let us hold hands with one another and sing." Whose hand are you holding? Jesus' hand? that of your friend? that of your former enemy?

What song are you singing together? Can you sing it now aloud or inwardly? Or can you write a song?

Jesus says, "My table is always here for you. You are all my beloved. Come to the table whenever you need it, whenever you feel me calling you. And bring with you in your heart anyone who needs the love and healing of this table. Now come, let us go forth."

Stand and stretch. Open your palms, giving thanks to God for the abundant table given to us forever. Gently massage your face and hands and go forth.

CHAPTER ELEVEN

Forgiveness
Fully Formed

In Christ, the there is here.

—Ancient saying

Is forgiveness really a journey? As I think about these stages of our inner release, other images and metaphors are rising.

The clear naming of our hurt, the safe space to feel our feeling, the choice to move away from force into power, the growing power to make firm choices, the beginnings of mercy that sees the wound in the other, seeing through God's eyes the underlying splendor within the other, the bringing of the passionate peace, claiming Christ's strength in the midst of opposition, the joyful advance with Christ to transform the darkness: All these aspects of forgiveness are intertwined, one part nourished by another. These characteristics make forgiveness feel living, organic, active, and moving.

Rather than a journey, I could speak of a great tree with its interconnecting, interdependent roots, trunk, branches, leaves, fruit, seeds. After all, the lampstand in the ancient Temple's holy of holies was shaped like the tree of life.

I am also thinking of a vast, unfolding blossom in that new mysteries are revealed to us as its heart slowly opens.

We could think of our forgiveness as a great garden that we explore or a beautiful, complex house with winding passages and unexpected rooms.

To some, forgiveness might seem like a spiral of light in which they circle back to former stages but always from a different angle and perspective.

Might forgiveness come to us as the early dawn does, slowly expanding its light to all the most hidden places of the valleys and mountains?

Some may experience forgiveness in their lives as a river, fed by new streams, constantly widening.

> Then the angel showed me the river of the water of life, bright as crystal, flowing from the throne of God and of the Lamb through the middle of the street of the city. On either side of the river, is the tree of life . . . and the leaves of the tree are for the healing of the nations. (Revelation 22:1-2)

Some may find forgiveness like the growth of a child to full maturity through the various stages of human development.

Our widening, deepening experience of forgiveness may seem like all these (and other) images at different times.

For myself, as I conclude this journey, this writing, I begin to realize that what we are dimly perceiving is far greater than any of these varying metaphors. A *person* is increasingly revealed to us: a face, a being, a personality who has never gone away, who has been forever with us, whose name is mercy, whose presence *is* the empowerment of forgiveness, release. That for which we have been looking somewhere down the road, a condition of love called forgiveness, a mountaintop of release, is at this moment enfolding us in the presence of God through the living Jesus.

We are not so much called to a journey as to a relationship, a bonding (the opposite of bondage) with one whose passion was to set us free:

> He unrolled the scroll and found the place where it was written:
> "The Spirit of the Lord is upon me,
> because he has anointed me to bring good news to the poor.
> He has sent me to proclaim release to the captives
> and recovery of sight to the blind,
> to let the oppressed go free,
> to proclaim the year of the Lord's favor." (Luke 4:17-19)

The *year of the Lord's favor* refers to the Jubilee year in Israel. It was celebrated every fifty years and announced by the blowing of the shofar, the ram's horn. In theory at least in this year all debts were forgiven, all slaves and prisoners set free, the fertile land given a year's rest, and property that had exchanged hands was returned to the original owners.

In effect Jesus is saying that the time of restoration, forgiveness, release exists now, in God's heart. We do not have to wait for fifty years; the Jubilee is already embodied in Jesus. The shofar this moment blows its proclamation of forgiveness and release, and it sounds through our bodies, our daily lives, our communities.

Forgiving from the heart is not easy. Over and over we may need to return to the earlier stages, and it may take a long time for us to feel and experience its fullness and completeness. But within these stages, no matter where we are, the living Christ is telling us that forgiveness is already complete in all fullness within him. Though we know forgiveness only dimly, this power is embodied in the risen Jesus and walks with us.

When we are full of hate, the living Jesus loves through us; when we are tired, the living Jesus breathes the breath of life into us. When we are numb and cannot pray at all, the living Jesus prays for us, in us, and through us. We are reminded that we do not create forgiveness. It already exists. We join it, abide in it, and slowly we come to life.

The newspaper today tells of another heartrending child abuse case. Unbearable! I may have just written a book about forgiveness, but at the moment I cannot even begin to think of mercy for that abuser. I can't even begin to form a prayer for the wounded person or hidden angel within the abuser. Perhaps later I will feel within me the empowerment of envisioning prayer for the abuser.

But at this moment I need and can take only one thing. For now what I need is to hold fast to the living Christ who already holds me forever. At this moment, what I need is to hear that inner voice saying: "I have them both in my hands, that child and his abuser. I see their hearts, and I know their wounds. I share and bear the pain. Your anger is also mine. But the healing and resurrection of both the wounded and the wounder live also in my heart.

"All that is needed for mercy and forgiveness surrounds you. In the right time you will feel it, pray for it. When you are with me, you are already within its flow. With me the there is here.

"I am with you always. Breathe my breath. Lean your full heavy heart on my strength in this dark place. Let me pray in you, for you, and through you."

Forgiveness is a person. Forgiveness has a face. Forgiveness itself is holding me now.

> Yea, thro' life, death, thro' sorrow and thro' sinning
> He shall suffice me, for he hath sufficed:
> Christ is the end, for Christ was the beginning,
> Christ the beginning, for the end is Christ.[1]

Notes

~

Chapter One

1. Sandra M. Flaherty, *Woman, Why Do You Weep? Spirituality for Survivors of Childhood Sexual Abuse* (New York: Paulist Press, 1992), 140.

Chapter Three

1. Dennis Linn, Sheila Fabricant Linn, and Matthew Linn, *Don't Forgive Too Soon* (New York: Paulist Press,1997), 42.
2. Rachel N. Remen, *Kitchen Table Wisdom* (New York: Riverhead Press, 1996), 30.
3. Ibid., 31.
4. Emilie P. Rose, *Reaching for the Light: A Guide for Ritual Abuse Survivors and Their Therapists* (Cleveland, Ohio: Pilgrim Press, 1996), 146–47.
5. Frederic W. H. Myers, *Saint Paul* (London: Macmillan, 1898), 5, 17.

Chapter Four

1. Walter Wink, *Engaging the Powers: Discernment and Resistance in a World of Domination* (Minneapolis: Fortress Press, 1992), 176–77.

Chapter Five

1. Pamela Cooper-White, *The Cry of Tamar: Violence against Women and the Church's Response* (Minneapolis: Fortress Press, 1995), 261.
2. Patricia Evans, *The Verbally Abusive Relationship: How to Recognize It and How to Respond* (Holbrook, Mass.: Bob Adams, 1992), 118–19.

Chapter Six

1. Andrew Sung Park, *The Wounded Heart of God: The Asian Concept of Han and the Christian Doctrine of Sin* (Nashville, Tenn.: Abingdon Press, 1993), 121, 123.
2. Linda H. Hollies, *Taking Back My Yesterdays: Lessons in Forgiving and Moving Forward with Your Life* (Cleveland, Ohio: Pilgrim Press, 1997), 2–5.

Chapter Eight

1. For further discussion on this issue, see my book *Feed My Shepherds,* chapter eight: "Our Greatest Flaw, Our Greatest Gift" (Nashville, Tenn.: Upper Room Books, 1998).
2. Brennan Manning, *A Stranger to Self-Hatred: A Glimpse of Jesus* (Denville, N.J.: Dimension Books, 1982), 103.

Chapter Nine

1. John S. Mogabgab, "Editor's Introduction," *Weavings: A Journal of the Christian Spiritual Life* 12, no. 6 (November/December 1997), 2.
2. Agnes Sanford, *Behold Your God* (Saint Paul, Minn.: Macalester Park Publishing, 1959), 125.

Chapter Ten

1. Herbert Musurillo, *The Acts of the Christian Martyrs* (Oxford: Oxford University Press, 1972), 125, 127.
2. William Blake, *The Works of William Blake* (Roslyn, N.Y.: Black's Readers Service, 1953), 69.

Chapter Eleven

1. Myers, *Saint Paul,* 53.

Other Titles by
Flora Slosson Wuellner
from Upper Room Books

*Feed My Shepherds: Spiritual Healing and Renewal for Those
in Christian Leadership (0-8358-0845-9)*

*Heart of Healing, Heart of Light: Encountering God Who
Shares and Heals Our Pain (0-8358-0666-9)*

Prayer and Our Bodies (0-8358-0568-9)

*Prayer, Fear, and Our Powers: Finding Our Healing, Release,
and Growth in Christ (0-8358-0597-2)*

Prayer, Stress, and Our Inner Wounds (0-8358-0501-8)

*Release: Healing from Wounds of Family, Church, and
Community (0-8358-0775-4)*